# COOKING
# Italian

## The Confident Cooking Promise of Success

Welcome to the world of Confident Cooking,
where recipes are double-tested by our team
of home economists to achieve a high standard
of success—and delicious results every time.

**bay books**

# C O N T E

Spaghetti with Chicken Meatballs, page 33

Rolled Capsicums, page 47

Pork with Mustard and Cream Sauce, page 71

Carrot and Pumpkin Risotto, page 88

Seafood Soup, page 18

Chocolate Ricotta Tart, page 104

The Publisher thanks the following for their assistance in the photography for this book: The Nicholas Agency; Ventura Design.

All recipes are double-tested by our team of home economists. When we test our recipes, we rate them for ease of preparation. The following cookery ratings are on the recipes in this book, making them easy to use and understand.

A single Cooking with Confidence symbol indicates a recipe that is simple and generally quick to make—perfect for beginners.

Two symbols indicate the need for just a little more care and a little more time.

Three symbols indicate special dishes that need more investment in time, care and patience—but the results are worth it.

### IMPORTANT
Those who might be at risk from the effects of salmonella food poisoning (the elderly, pregnant women, young children and those suffering from immune deficiency diseases) should consult their doctor with any concerns about eating raw eggs.

Mussels in Two Sauces, page 67

Olive and Onion Tart, page 52

# The taste of Italy

It is an understatement to say that food is important to the Italians. They love to eat, and meals are prepared with great pride and affection as a daily highlight of the family life which is central to their whole culture. The Italian style of cooking we know today developed from many isolated regional cuisines throughout the country. Though there were common threads, the geography, climate and outside influences of each region made them all unique. Pasta and risotto may have been known throughout Italy, but the ingredients which flavoured them varied, depending on which region you were dining in at the time. Generally, cheese and butter still feature prominently in northern Italy, reflecting the close proximity to the dairy-loving neighbours of Switzerland and Austria. Moving south, olive oil, tomatoes and fish define the Mediterranean diet.

Many regions boast a famous speciality, the production of which is a fiercely guarded tradition handed down through generations and sometimes even protected by law. Parmesan cheese is a good example of this. Although today there are very many varieties available, the best is widely accepted to be Parmigiano Reggiano, which comes from a strictly defined area around the city of Parma (also famous for its ham). Reggiano broadcasts its authenticity with its name emblazoned along the wide rind. The fact that many dishes are named for the city or region where they were first eaten, such as Spaghetti Napolitana (Naples) or Bolognese (Bologna), indicates the extent to which the Italians define themselves by their culinary heritage.

So where does this leave us today? Fortunate indeed, to be able to enjoy the best of all that Italy has to offer. Italian restaurants have been popular for many years and, despite a proliferation of questionable pizza and pasta joints, remain at the cutting edge of chic. And not just for special occasions—Italian food is now part of our day-to-day lives. We crunch biscotti with our morning caffe latte, grab a focaccia filled with mozzarella and prosciutto for lunch, and enjoy a bowl of spaghetti with pesto for dinner.

Cooking Italian food at home is an easy and enjoyable experience, with the vast majority of ingredients now usually available at the supermarket and greengrocer.

The key to good Italian food is freshness. There are no second bests and no Italian cook would even contemplate preparing a dish without the best-quality, freshest ingredients. And if they aren't available, well then make something else instead. While pantry staples such as tinned tomatoes, anchovies, dried pasta, arborio rice and olive oil provide the backbone, fresh vegetables and herbs lift the dishes into the sublime. The Italian cook's favourite herbs are generally used fresh, often gathered from the surrounding area in great basketfuls. Basil is widely used to enhance tomato and pasta dishes and Italian parsley is the flat-leafed variety with a pungent aroma and flavour. Vegetables such as zucchini, eggplant, tomatoes, artichokes and capsicums are as delicious as they are good for you.

And, speaking of healthy, the 'Mediterranean' diet has been touted endlessly as the ideal, with olive oil now being revered rather than reviled. Fortunately, it is not so worthy as to be dull and unappetizing, but consists of dishes which combine those two truly mouth-watering ingredients—health *and* happiness.

Although today we have become accustomed to pizza or pasta as a full meal in itself, the Italian dinner in its glorious entirety is a true work of art. The opening spread is the antipasto, meaning 'before the meal', intended not to satisfy but merely titillate the palate. An antipasto platter can be an elaborate array of marinated seafood, aromatic salads and frittata, or a simple plate of prosciutto with ripe figs and juicy melon slices. The only golden rule, as always, is that freshness abounds. To follow, come the *primi piatti* or 'first plates'. These can vary endlessly, but will more often than not consist of a hearty Italian soup (Minestrone being by far the best known) or pasta, polenta or risotto. We are, on the whole, unused to filling up on starch or carbohydrate before the main dish, but as a tradition in a country where meat may have been scarce or costly, it makes great sense. It also goes to explain the wonderful simplicity of Italian meat or fish dishes.

Vegetarians and non-red-meat eaters fare well with Italian cuisine. Staples such as polenta, rice and pasta are filling and satisfying and, when dressed up with beans, seafood and fresh vegetables, provide great nutrition. The vast majority of Italian meals are finished off with a simple piece of fresh fruit, but to balance all this healthiness, the Italians have also let their national sweet tooth run riot and devised a vast array of wicked desserts, cakes and biscuits. Their gelato and other ice confections, such as Granita and Cassata, are world-renowned. Admittedly, Tiramisu may have been done to death in all the fashionable restaurants around town, but who cares? Like all Italian food, it still tastes wonderful.

# Glossary of Ingredients

Most of the ingredients for Italian cooking are well-known to us, but there are a few which have come into vogue only in the last few years. The majority are available in the supermarket or you may have to make a trip to the delicatessen. The golden rule is to always buy the best quality you can afford.

### ANCHOVIES
A small fish from the herring family with slightly oily flesh and a strong flavour. Anchovies can be eaten fresh, although they are rarely found outside Mediterranean fishing ports as the fish are delicate and need to be eaten or processed quickly. They are widely available as salted fillets marinated in oil, sold in jars or cans.

### ARBORIO RICE
Arborio rice derives its name from a small village in the Piedmont region in northern Italy where it is grown. It has a short, pearly grain and is used in both sweet and savoury dishes.
Arborio rice is particularly suited to making risotto—the rice absorbs a large amount of cooking liquid and becomes tender and creamy but not too soft.

### ARTICHOKE HEARTS
The fleshy centres or 'hearts' of the thistly artichoke head. These are available whole or quartered, canned or in jars, in marinade or brine.

### BALSAMIC VINEGAR
A richly flavoured, dark-coloured vinegar. This has a bitter-sweet taste, a slightly syrupy consistency and is used in salad dressings, sauces or as a meat marinade. Balsamic vinegar is made in Modena, Italy, from unfermented

Trebbiano (white) grapes. It is aged in wooden casks for no less than five years and sometimes up to a hundred. Price and quality vary greatly and are dependent on the age.

### BOCCONCINI
Traditionally shaped in balls, like a smaller version of Mozzarella cheese and often referred to as 'baby mozzarella'. Originally made in southern Italy from water buffalo milk, but now made using cows milk. This fresh, unripened cheese takes 24 hours to make, is milky white, soft and has a slightly sweet flavour. To keep it moist, it should be stored in the whey in which it is sold.

### BORLOTTI BEAN
A slightly kidney-shaped bean which is a pale, pinky brown colour with darker speckled markings. It has a smooth texture and a ham-like flavour when cooked and is used in soups, stews, casseroles or salads. Available dried, canned or fresh in season.

### CANNELLINI BEAN
A white, slightly kidney-shaped bean, also known as Italian haricot bean or white kidney bean. Mildly flavoured and slightly fluffy in texture when cooked, these are good all-purpose beans for use in soups, casseroles, stews and salads. Available dried or canned.

### CAPERS
The unopened, olive-green flower buds of a prickly shrub native to the Mediterranean, the Middle East and northern Africa. These are sold in a seasoned vinegar or packed in salt. Capers have a sharp sour taste and are used in sauces, salad dressings and often as an accompaniment to smoked salmon. Salted capers should be washed thoroughly before use.

### FONTINA
Prized by connoisseurs as being among the six greatest cheeses of the world. Fontina is a semi-hard flat round cheese with a smooth creamy texture and slightly sweet nutty flavour. Traditionally served in Italian dishes, melted over polenta.

### GNOCCHI
Small soft Italian dumplings made from semolina or potato dough and sometimes flavoured with spinach, pumpkin or cheese. Not to be confused with the dried pasta of the same name.

### MASCARPONE
A fresh unripened soft cream cheese with a slightly sour flavour, originally from Lombardy. It can be eaten fresh with fruit, and is widely used in Italian cooking, usually in desserts and cheesecakes.

## MOZZARELLA

A smooth white cheese with a mild, slightly sweet flavour. Often eaten fresh in Italy, in a simple salad with tomatoes and olives, but best known for its use on pizzas.

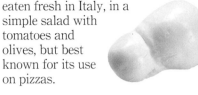

## OLIVE OIL

A pale yellow to deep green, mono-unsaturated oil made from pressed olives. It has a fruity flavour and is used for frying and in salad dressings.

Extra virgin olive oil is a cold pressed oil from the first pressing of the olives. It has a strong flavour and is deep green in colour.

Virgin olive oil is from the second pressing of the olives and is slightly milder in flavour and a little lighter in colour.

Light olive oil is made from subsequent pressings and has usually been heated in the extraction process. The flavour is very mild and it is light in colour—not lower in fat, as is sometimes assumed from the name.

## PANCETTA

Unsmoked bacon, from the belly of the pig, that has been cured with spices. It is usually sold rolled into a sausage shape and cut into very thin slices.

## PARMESAN

A very hard cows milk cheese with a strong sharp taste and grainy texture. Widely used in Italian cooking, either grated in dishes or as shavings to garnish. Always buy Parmesan in a chunk from a delicatessen and grate it as you need it rather than using the ready grated packet Parmesan. The variety which is stamped 'Parmigiano Reggiano' on the rind is the most superior Parmesan—this is, of course, reflected in the price, but it is worth it.

## PECORINO

A cooked curd sheeps milk cheese, available in two varieties: Romano, a hard grating cheese similar to Parmesan, and Fresco, a young, softer version that can be served as a table cheese.

## PINE NUTS

The small, slender, soft golden seed shed by the fully mature cone of certain types of pine tree. Traditionally used for stuffings, salads, cakes and biscuits, but best known as a key ingredient in pesto sauce.

## POLENTA

Polenta is another name for cornmeal, and is also the name of the dish made from the cornmeal. The dish is a thick porridge which is eaten with casseroles and stews or, with the addition of Parmesan cheese, is left to set firm and then grilled or fried.

## PROSCIUTTO

A cured Italian ham taken from the hind of the pig. Aged for eight to ten months, it is sliced wafer thin and may be cooked or served raw. Prosciutto di Parma is the classic Italian ham, produced from pigs fattened on the whey left over from making the local cheese, Parmigiano Reggiano.

## RADICCHIO

A deep purple, lettuce-like vegetable with a sharp, bitter flavour. Used in salads or braised or grilled and served with meat or chicken.

## RICOTTA

A soft, moist white cheese with a slightly sweet flavour. Used in savoury spreads, or as a dessert with fruit or as a filling for cheesecakes.

## ROCKET (ARUGULA)

A salad green with slender deep green leaves. This has a peppery, bitter flavour that complements other leaves in a mixed green salad. The older and larger the leaf, the stronger its flavour.

## ROMANO

A hard grating cheese usually made from cows milk, this has a similar texture and taste to Parmesan. When made with sheeps milk it is called Pecorino Romano.

## SUN-DRIED TOMATOES

Widely available either dry and loosely packed or in jars in oil. The dry variety need to be rehydrated before use—cover with boiling water and leave for about 10 minutes. If buying sun-dried tomatoes in oil, choose the variety in olive oil—you can then use this for cooking as it will have extra flavour.

# ANTIPASTO

What more delicious way to whet the appetite than with a colourful antipasto platter? The name translates literally as 'before the meal' and the tradition arose from the lengthy banquets of the Roman Empire. These recipes serve 4–8 people, depending on how many dishes you prepare.

## CANNELLINI BEAN SALAD

Rinse and drain a 425 g (13½ oz) can cannellini beans and toss together with 1 tablespoon finely chopped red onion, 1 chopped tomato, 3 sliced anchovy fillets, 2 teaspoons finely chopped basil leaves, 2 teaspoons extra virgin olive oil and 1 teaspoon balsamic vinegar. Season to taste.

## ARTICHOKE FRITTATA

Heat 30 g (1 oz) butter in a non-stick frying pan, add 2 small sliced leeks and 1 sliced clove of garlic and cook until soft. Spread evenly over the bottom of the pan. Lightly beat 6 eggs and season with salt and black pepper. Slice 100 g (3⅓ oz) bottled artichoke hearts. Pour the eggs into the pan and arrange the artichoke slices on top. Sprinkle with 1 teaspoon chopped fresh tarragon. Cook over low heat until set (this will take about 10 minutes), shaking the pan occasionally to evenly distribute the egg. Place under a hot grill to lightly brown the top. Cut into wedges and drizzle with a little lemon juice to serve.

*Clockwise from left: Cannellini Bean Salad; Artichoke Frittata; Ricotta Spread; Italian Meatballs; Marinated Mushrooms*

## RICOTTA SPREAD

Beat 200 g (6½ oz) ricotta with 2 tablespoons lemon juice until smooth and then fold in 3 tablespoons sliced black olives and 1 tablespoon chopped sun-dried tomatoes. Pile into a serving bowl and sprinkle with 1 tablespoon chopped chives. Serve with crusty Italian bread.

## ITALIAN MEATBALLS

Combine 250 g (8 oz) lean beef mince, a grated small onion, 1 crushed clove of garlic, ½ cup (40 g/1⅓ oz) fresh white breadcrumbs, 3 tablespoons chopped black olives, 1 teaspoon dried oregano, 1 tablespoon finely chopped parsely and salt and black pepper to taste. Mix together thoroughly with your hands. Form teaspoonsful of mixture into balls. Heat a little oil in a frying pan and cook the meatballs in batches until well browned.

## MARINATED MUSHROOMS

Wipe 315 g (10 oz) small button mushrooms clean with damp paper towels and cut in half (never wash mushrooms by soaking in water or they will become soggy). Place the mushrooms in a bowl with 3 finely sliced spring onions and 1 finely sliced celery stick, then gently mix together. Stir through 1 crushed clove of garlic, 3 tablespoons extra virgin olive oil, 2 tablespoons lemon juice and 1 tablespoon finely chopped chives. Refrigerate for about 4 hours for the flavours to combine, but allow to return to room temperature before serving.

**Note:** For a delicious mushroom salad, use the same recipe for Marinated Mushrooms but place the mushrooms in the base of a large salad bowl. Top with torn lettuce leaves or a mixture of torn salad leaves and toss well just before serving. You may need to make more dressing (marinade), depending on the amount of lettuce in your salad.

# ANTIPASTO

### CARPACCIO

Take a 400 g (12²/3 oz) piece of beef eye fillet and remove all the visible fat and sinew. Freeze for 1–2 hours, until firm but not frozen solid (this makes the meat easier to slice thinly). Cut paper thin slices of beef with a large, sharp knife. Arrange on a serving platter and allow to return to room temperature. Drizzle with 1 tablespoon extra virgin olive oil, then scatter with torn rocket leaves, black olives cut into slivers and shavings of Parmesan cheese. Serve at room temperature.

## PASTA FRITTATA

Cook 300 g (9²/3 oz) spaghetti in a large pan of boiling water, until just tender but still retaining a little bite, then drain well. Whisk 4 eggs together in a large bowl, then add ¹/2 cup (50 g/1²/3 oz) finely grated Parmesan cheese, 2 tablespoons chopped fresh parsley and salt and freshly ground black pepper. Add the spaghetti and toss together until well coated. Melt 1 tablespoon butter in a large frying pan and add the spaghetti mixture. Cover and cook over low heat until the base is crisp and golden. Slide the frittata onto a plate, melt another tablespoon of butter in the pan and flip the frittata back in to cook the other side (do not cover or the Frittata will not get a crisp finish). Serve warm, cut into wedges.

## STUFFED CHERRY TOMATOES

Slice the tops from 16 cherry tomatoes, hollow out and discard the seeds. Turn upside-down and leave to drain for a few minutes. Beat together 50 g (1²/3 oz) each goats cheese and ricotta until smooth. Finely chop 2 slices prosciutto, discarding any fat, and mix with the cheeses. Season with salt and ground black pepper. Stuff into the tomatoes, using your fingers, and refrigerate until required.

## PROSCIUTTO WITH MELON

Cut a melon (rockmelon or honeydew) into thin wedges and remove the seeds. Wrap a slice of prosciutto around each piece of fruit, drizzle with a little extra virgin olive oil and grind some black pepper over each.

*From left: Carpaccio; Pasta Frittata; Stuffed Cherry Tomatoes; Prosciutto with Melon; Marinated Eggplant*

## MARINATED EGGPLANT

Cut 750 g (1¹/2 lb) slender eggplant into thick diagonal slices. Put in a colander and sprinkle well with salt. After 30 minutes, rinse and pat dry. Mix 3 tablespoons olive oil, 2 tablespoons balsamic vinegar, 2 crushed cloves of garlic and 1 finely chopped anchovy fillet; whisk until smooth and season to taste. Heat a little oil in a large non-stick frying pan and brown the eggplant on both sides. Place in a bowl, add the dressing and 2 tablespoons chopped parsley and toss. Marinate for 4 hours and serve at room temperature.

# SEAFOOD ANTIPASTO

### CHAR-GRILLED OCTOPUS

Combine 2/3 cup (170 ml/5$\frac{1}{2}$ fl oz) olive oil, 1/3 cup (10 g/ 1/3 oz) chopped fresh oregano, 1/3 cup (10 g/1/3 oz) chopped fresh parsley, 3 finely chopped small red chillies and 3 cloves of crushed garlic in a large bowl. Wash 1 kg (2 lb) baby octopus and dry well. Slit the head open and remove the gut. Grasp the body firmly and push the beak out with your index finger. Add the octopus to the oil mixture and marinate for 3–4 hours or overnight. Drain, reserving the marinade. Cook on a very hot barbecue or in a very hot pan for 3–5 minutes, or until the flesh turns white. Turn frequently and brush with the marinade during cooking.

### SCALLOP FRITTERS

Combine 6 lightly beaten eggs with 1/4 cup (25 g/3/4 oz) grated Parmesan, 3 cloves crushed garlic, 1 cup (125 g/4 oz) plain flour and 2 tablespoons each chopped fresh thyme and oregano. Mix well with a wooden spoon until smooth. Fold in 250 g (8 oz) cleaned and chopped scallops. Heat oil for shallow-frying until moderately hot. Pour quarter-cupfuls of batter into the hot oil and cook in batches for 4–5 minutes over moderate heat, until golden brown. Drain on paper towels and serve with mayonnaise or plain yoghurt.

### SARDINES IN VINE LEAVES

Place 12 fresh vine leaves in a large heatproof bowl and cover with boiling water. Leave for 2–3 minutes, rinse with cold water, drain and pat dry. If using vine leaves in brine, soak in cold water for 30 minutes, drain and pat dry. Preheat the oven to moderate 180°C (350°F/Gas 4). Heat 1 tablespoon olive oil in a frying pan and add 1 crushed clove of garlic, 1 finely chopped spring onion and 2 tablespoons pine nuts. Cook, stirring, until the pine nuts just begin to turn brown. Combine in a bowl with 3 tablespoons chopped parsley, 2 teaspoons finely grated lemon rind and 3 tablespoons fresh white breadcrumbs. Season with salt and freshly ground black pepper. Fill 12 sardine fillets with the breadcrumb mixture and wrap each in a vine leaf. Place in a single layer in a well greased baking dish. Drizzle with 2 tablespoons olive oil and bake for 30 minutes. Serve at room temperature, with mayonnaise flavoured with crushed garlic.

*From left: Char-grilled Octopus; Scallop Fritters; Sardines in Vine Leaves; Marinated Seafood; Smoked Cod Frittata with Rocket; Mussels with Crispy Prosciutto*

## MUSSELS WITH CRISPY PROSCIUTTO

Heat 1 tablespoon oil in a small frying pan. Add 1 finely chopped onion, 6 thin slices prosciutto, chopped, and 4 crushed cloves garlic. Cook until the prosciutto is crispy and the onion softened, then set aside. Add 1.5 kg (3 lb) cleaned mussels to a large pot of boiling water and cook for 5 minutes, discarding any that don't open. Remove the mussels from their shells, keeping half of each shell. Place two mussels on each half-shell and top with the prosciutto mixture. Combine 1/2 cup (50 g/1 2/3 oz) grated Parmesan and 1/2 cup (60 g/2 oz) grated Cheddar cheese and sprinkle over the prosciutto. Cook under a preheated grill until the cheese has melted and the mussels are warmed through.

## SMOKED COD FRITTATA WITH ROCKET

Place 500 g (1 lb) smoked cod in a pan with enough milk and water to cover. Bring to the boil, then reduce the heat and simmer for 3–4 minutes. Remove with a slotted spoon and flake the flesh. Whisk 8 eggs in a bowl. Add 1/2 cup (50 g/1 2/3 oz) grated Parmesan and 1/2 cup (60 g/2 oz) grated Cheddar cheese, 2 tablespoons chopped fresh thyme, 1/2 cup (30 g/1 oz) torn basil leaves and the fish. Mix to combine. Heat 2 tablespoons olive oil in a large heavy-based frying pan. Pour in the mixture and cook over medium heat for 5 minutes, or until nearly cooked. Place under a hot grill for 3–4 minutes, or until just set and lightly golden. Transfer to a large serving platter and pile 2 cups (40 g/1 1/3 oz) torn rocket leaves in the centre.

## MARINATED SEAFOOD

Slice 500 g (1 lb) small squid hoods into rings. Shell and devein 500 g (1 lb) raw prawns. Scrub and remove the beards from 500 g (1 lb) mussels, discarding any which are already open. Put 3 cups (750 ml/24 fl oz) water, 1/2 cup (125 ml/4 fl oz) white wine vinegar, 1/2 teaspoon of salt and 3 bay leaves in a large pan and bring to the boil. Add the squid and 500 g (1 lb) scallops, then reduce the heat to low and simmer for 2–3 minutes, or until the seafood has turned white. Remove the squid and scallops with a slotted spoon and place in a bowl. Repeat the process with the prawns, cooking until just pink. Return the liquid to the boil and add the mussels; cover, reduce the heat and simmer for about 3 minutes, until all the shells are open. Discard any mussels that haven't opened. Cool the mussels, remove the meat and add to the bowl. Whisk together 2 crushed cloves of garlic, 1/2 cup (125 ml/4 fl oz) extra virgin olive oil, 3 tablespoons lemon juice, 1 tablespoon white wine vinegar, 1 teaspoon Dijon mustard and 1 tablespoon chopped parsley. Pour over the seafood and toss well. Refrigerate for 1–2 hours and then serve on a bed of lettuce leaves.

**Note:** Any seafood can be used for this dish—the most important thing to remember is that seafood should never be overcooked or it will become tough. To make this dish more economical, substitute white fish fillets for most of the prawns and scallops. Poach the fish in the cooking liquid for a few minutes, drain immediately and cut into chunks. Toss carefully with the rest of the seafood in the dressing and garnish with a few cooked prawns and scallops.

# SOUPS AND STARTERS

### BRUSCHETTA WITH MEDITERRANEAN TOPPINGS

Preparation time: 20 minutes
Total cooking time: 15 minutes
Serves 4–6

*Capsicum Topping*
1 yellow capsicum
1 red capsicum
1 green capsicum

*Tomato and Basil Topping*
2 ripe tomatoes
1/4 cup (15 g/1/2 oz) shredded
    fresh basil
1 tablespoon extra virgin
    olive oil

12 slices crusty Italian bread
2 cloves garlic, halved
1/3 cup (80 ml/2³/4 fl oz) extra
    virgin olive oil
1 tablespoon chopped flat-leaf
    parsley

**1 To make Capsicum Topping:**
Cut the capsicums in half lengthways and remove the seeds and membrane. Flatten slightly and place, skin-side-up, under a hot grill until the skins are blackened. Cover with a tea towel or put the capsicums in a paper or plastic bag, seal and leave until cool. Peel away the skins and discard. Slice the flesh into strips.

**2 To make Tomato and Basil Topping:** Finely chop the tomatoes and combine in a bowl with the basil and olive oil. Season with freshly ground black pepper.

**3 To make Bruschetta:** Toast the bread slices and, while still hot, rub with the cut side of a garlic clove. Drizzle olive oil over each slice of bread and sprinkle with salt and plenty of freshly ground black pepper.

**4** Arrange the Capsicum Topping on top of half the bread slices; sprinkle with parsley. Arrange the Tomato and Basil Topping on the remaining slices of bread. Serve immediately.

### COOK'S FILE

**Note:** Extra virgin olive oil is produced from the first pressing of the olives. Using a superior oil in your cooking makes the difference between a good dish and a great one—always use the best-quality oil you can afford. 'Light' olive oil is from the last pressing and has a very mild flavour.

*Grill the capsicums until the skin is blackened, leave to cool, then peel.*

*Rub the hot toasted bruschetta with the cut side of the garlic clove.*

## BROCCOLI AND PINE NUT SOUP

Preparation time: 10 minutes
Total cooking time: 30 minutes
Serves 6

30 g (1 oz) butter
1 onion, finely chopped
6 cups (1.5 litres) chicken stock
750 g (1¹/2 lb) fresh broccoli

¹/3 cup (50 g/1²/3 oz) pine nuts
extra pine nuts, to serve

**1** Melt the butter in a large pan and cook the onion over moderate heat until soft but not browned. Add the stock and bring to the boil.
**2** Remove the florets from the broccoli and set aside. Chop the broccoli stalks and add to the pan. Reduce the heat, cover and simmer for 15 minutes. Add the florets and simmer, uncovered, for 10 minutes, or until the florets are tender. Allow to cool completely.
**3** Add the pine nuts and blend until smooth in a food processor (you may need to blend in batches, depending on the size of your processor). Season to taste with salt and pepper, then gently reheat. Sprinkle with extra pine nuts to serve. Delicious with toasted foccacia, drizzled with extra virgin olive oil.

*Cook the onion until soft and then add the chicken stock.*

*Remove the florets from the broccoli and chop the stalks into even-sized pieces.*

*Let the soup cool, to prevent burns, then process with the pine nuts.*

## MINESTRONE

Preparation time: 30 minutes +
  overnight soaking
Total cooking time: 2 hours 45 minutes
Serves 6–8

250 g (8 oz) dried borlotti beans
2 tablespoons oil
2 onions, chopped
2 cloves garlic, crushed
3 rashers bacon, chopped
4 egg tomatoes, peeled and
  chopped
3 tablespoons chopped parsley

9 cups (2.25 litres) beef or
  vegetable stock
3 tablespoons red wine
1 carrot, peeled and chopped
1 swede, peeled and diced
2 potatoes, peeled and diced
3 tablespoons tomato paste
2 zucchini, sliced
1/2 cup (80 g/2²/3 oz) peas
1/2 cup (80 g/2²/3 oz) small
  macaroni
Parmesan and pesto, to serve

**1** Soak the borlotti beans in water
overnight and drain. Add to a pan of
boiling water, simmer for 15 minutes

and drain. Heat the oil in a large
heavy-based pan and cook the onion,
garlic and bacon, stirring, until the
onion is soft and the bacon golden.
**2** Add the tomato, parsley, borlotti
beans, stock and red wine. Simmer,
covered, over low heat for 2 hours.
Add the carrot, swede, potato and
tomato paste, cover and simmer for a
further 15–20 minutes.
**3** Add the zucchini, peas and pasta.
Cover and simmer for 10–15 minutes,
or until the vegetables and macaroni
are tender. Season to taste with salt
and pepper and serve topped with
grated Parmesan and a little pesto.

*Soak the borlotti beans in a bowl of water
overnight and then drain.*

*Use a sharp knife to peel and dice the
swede and other vegetables.*

*Stir the onion and bacon over the heat
until soft and golden.*

17

## SEAFOOD SOUP

Preparation time: 40 minutes
Total cooking time: 1 hour 40 minutes
Serves 6

800 g (1 lb 10 oz) baby octopus
155 g (5 oz) small cleaned
    calamari tubes
500 g (1 lb) firm fish fillets
12 small mussels in shells
1 tablespoon olive oil
2 small onions, sliced
1 anchovy fillet, finely chopped
3 large ripe tomatoes, skinned
    and finely chopped
3 fresh mint leaves, torn
2 bay leaves
1/2 cup (125 ml/4 fl oz) dry
    white wine
315 g (10 oz) frozen peas
12 raw king prawns, shelled and
    deveined with tails intact
2 tablespoons lemon juice

*Garlic Bread*
6 slices crusty Italian bread
1 clove garlic, halved

*Parsley Pesto*
1 cup (20 g/2/3 oz) firmly packed
    flat-leaf parsley leaves
2 cloves garlic, chopped
2 tablespoons lemon juice
2 tablespoons olive oil

**1** Remove the heads and beaks from the octopus and cut the tentacles into smaller portions. Cut the calamari tubes into rings. Put the octopus in a large pan of boiling water, partially cover the pan and leave to simmer for 30 minutes. Add the calamari rings and simmer for 15–20 minutes, or until tender. Drain thoroughly.

**2** Cut the fish fillets into bite-sized portions. Scrub the mussel shells and remove their beards. Refrigerate all the seafood on separate plates.

**3** Heat the oil in a large pan and cook the onion over moderate heat until starting to colour. Stir in the anchovy, tomatoes, mint and bay leaves, wine, 1.5 litres water, and salt and pepper, to taste. Bring to the boil, lower the heat and simmer for 20 minutes.

**4 To make Garlic Bread:** Preheat the oven to 160°C (315°F/Gas 2–3). Put the bread on a baking tray in a single layer. Bake for 20 minutes, or until crisp, turning once. Rub each slice of bread with the cut garlic.

**5 To make Parsley Pesto:** Put the parsley, garlic, lemon juice and olive oil in a food processor. Process into a fine paste and season to taste with salt and pepper. Cover and refrigerate until ready to serve.

**6** Just before serving, bring the soup back to the boil and add the peas, mussels and fish. Reduce the heat to simmer, uncovered, for 3 minutes or until the mussels start to open. Add the prawns, octopus and calamari. Bring back to the boil, then reduce the heat and simmer for 2–3 minutes, or until all the seafood is tender. Stir in the lemon juice and discard any unopened mussels. Place a slice of Garlic Bread in each serving bowl and ladle Seafood Soup over the top. Serve the Parsley Pesto separately.

### COOK'S FILE

**Note:** To remove the beak from the octopus, turn the head inside out and push the beak (the dark hard bit) up firmly—it will pop out. The seafood, stock and bread can all be prepared a few hours in advance and the soup completed just before serving.

*Remove the heads and beaks from the octopus and cut the tentacles into pieces.*

*Cut the fish fillets into bite-sized pieces. Choose skinless fillets.*

*Add the tomatoes, mint leaves, bay leaves, water, wine and seasoning.*

*Bake the bread in a single layer, turning over after 10 minutes.*

*Put the parsley, garlic, lemon juice, oil and salt and pepper in a food processor.*

*Bring the soup to the boil, then simmer until the mussels begin to open.*

19

## BAKED RICOTTA

Preparation time: 15 minutes +
  overnight chilling
Total cooking time: 20 minutes
Serves 8

1 egg white
750 g (1¹/2 lb) fresh ricotta
  cheese, well drained
60 g (2 oz) sun-dried tomatoes
  in oil, drained and chopped
cracked black pepper
2 tablespoons chopped flat-leaf
  parsley
¹/2 teaspoon finely grated lemon
  rind
1 clove garlic, crushed
1 tablespoon extra virgin olive oil

**1** Preheat the oven to 180°C (350°F/Gas 4). Line the base of a 20 cm (8 inch) round shallow cake tin with foil and brush well with olive oil. Beat the egg white with a fork until frothy. Add the ricotta and mix thoroughly. Put half the mixture in the tin and spread evenly over the base. Scatter with the tomato and cracked pepper, spoon the remainder of the ricotta over the top and smooth the surface.
**2** Put the parsley, lemon rind and garlic in a bowl and mix well. Sprinkle over the ricotta, top with extra cracked pepper and then drizzle with oil. Brush a circle of foil with oil and place, oil-side-down, over the ricotta. Bake for 20 minutes, or until lightly set. Remove the foil.
**3** Leave to cool in the tin, then cover with foil and refrigerate overnight. Carefully turn out onto a tray, remove the foil and then cover with a plate and invert so that the parsley is uppermost. Serve in wedges at room temperature as an entrée, garnished with rocket leaves and black olives, or as part of an antipasto.

COOK'S FILE

**Hint:** The best way to thoroughly drain ricotta is to leave it in a colander overnight, weighed down with a can or plate. Put a large bowl underneath to catch the liquid.
**Variation:** Try sun-dried capsicum instead of tomatoes. Drizzle the oil from the tomatoes or capsicum on top, instead of virgin olive oil.

*To drain ricotta, leave it in a colander over a bowl and weigh down with a can.*

*Scatter the chopped tomatoes and cracked pepper over the ricotta.*

*Lightly oil a circle of foil and place it, oil-side-down, over the ricotta.*

## PARMESAN PEARS

Preparation time: 15 minutes
Total cooking time: 10 minutes
Serves 6

3 firm ripe pears
40 g (1⅓ oz) butter
6 thin slices pancetta, finely
   chopped
2 spring onions, finely sliced

¾ cup (60 g/2 oz) fresh white
   breadcrumbs
⅓ cup (35 g/1¼ oz) grated
   Parmesan

**1** Cut the pears in half and remove the cores with a melon baller or tea-spoon. Melt the butter in a frying pan. Brush the pears with a little melted butter and place, cut-side-up, on an oven tray. Put under a preheated grill for 4 minutes, or until heated through.

**2** Add the pancetta and onions to the remaining butter in the pan. Cook until the onions are soft but not brown. Add the breadcrumbs and black pepper to taste.

**3** Scatter the pancetta mixture over the pears, sprinkle with Parmesan and grill until golden brown. Serve warm as an entrée, or with roast chicken.

### COOK'S FILE

**Note:** Nashi pears are also suitable.

*A melon baller is ideal for cutting out the cores of the pears.*

*Cook the pancetta and spring onions until soft. Add the breadcrumbs and pepper.*

*Sprinkle the Parmesan over the pears and grill until golden brown.*

21

## ROCKET, GRAPE AND WALNUT SALAD

Preparation time: 15 minutes + chilling
Total cooking time: Nil
Serves 6

1 butter lettuce
1 radicchio
155 g (5 oz) rocket
1 cup (185 g/6 oz) green
    seedless grapes

½ cup (60 g/2 oz) broken
    walnuts, toasted

*Dressing*
⅓ cup (80 ml/2¾ fl oz) extra
    virgin olive oil
1 tablespoon lemon juice
2 teaspoons wholegrain mustard
freshly ground black pepper
1 tablespoon chopped chives

**1** Wash the lettuce, radicchio and rocket, then dry the leaves gently but thoroughly. Chill until crisp in an airtight container or plastic bag in the refrigerator. Arrange with the grapes in a large salad bowl or serving dish. Scatter with walnuts.
**2 To make Dressing:** Whisk together the oil, lemon juice, mustard and pepper. Add the chives.
**3** Drizzle the dressing over the salad and serve.

**COOK'S FILE**

**Hint:** Use the best oil you can afford.

*Wash the lettuce, radicchio and rocket leaves under cold running water.*

*Put the leaves in plastic bags or an airtight container and chill in the fridge.*

*Whisk together the oil, mustard, lemon juice and pepper to make a dressing.*

## PUMPKIN AND BORLOTTI BEAN SOUP

Preparation time: 20 minutes +
    overnight soaking
Total cooking time: 2 hours 10 minutes
Serves 4–6

350 g (11¼ oz) dried borlotti
    beans
1 kg (2 lb) butternut pumpkin
    pieces, skin and seeds removed
2 large potatoes, peeled and
    chopped
2 litres chicken stock
1 tablespoon olive oil

1 red onion, chopped
2 cloves garlic, finely chopped
1 celery stick, sliced
10 fresh sage leaves, chopped
½ teaspoon finely cracked
    black pepper

**1** Soak the beans in cold water overnight or for 8 hours, then rinse and drain. Put in a large saucepan, cover with water and simmer over gentle heat for 1½ hours, or until tender. Remove and drain.
**2** Place the pumpkin and potato pieces in a large saucepan and pour in the chicken stock. Bring to the boil, then reduce the heat and simmer for 35–40 minutes, or until soft. Remove from the heat and drain, reserving the liquid. Roughly mash the pumpkin and potatoes with a fork, then return to the pan with the reserved liquid. Stir in the beans.
**3** Heat the oil in a small frying pan, add the onion, garlic and celery and fry for 2–3 minutes. Add to the soup with the sage and pepper and heat through. Serve hot with crusty Italian bread.

**COOK'S FILE**

**Hint:** Ready-made chicken stock in a tetra pack is very convenient but can be salty—use half stock, half water.

*Put the beans in a large bowl of cold water and leave to soak overnight.*

*Roughly mash the potato and pumpkin with a fork, then return to the liquid.*

*Fry the onion, garlic and celery and then add to the soup.*

*Rocket, Grape and Walnut Salad (top) and Pumpkin and Borlotti Bean Soup*

# CLASSIC PASTA SAUCES

## BOLOGNESE

**1** Heat 2 tablespoons oil in a large pan and add 1 onion, 1 carrot and 1 celery stick, all diced. Cook over low heat for 10 minutes, stirring occasionally.

**2** Add 2 crushed cloves of garlic and cook for 1 more minute. Increase the heat slightly, add 500 g (1 lb) of beef mince and cook until well browned. Break up any lumps of meat with a fork as it cooks.

**3** Pour in 2 cups (500 ml/16 fl oz) beef stock, 1½ cups (375 ml/12 fl oz) red wine, two 425 g (13½ oz) cans crushed peeled tomatoes, 2 tablespoons chopped fresh parsley and 2 teaspoons sugar.

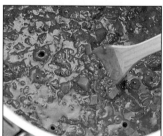

**4** Bring to the boil, then reduce the heat and simmer uncovered for 1½ hours, stirring occasionally, until reduced and thickened. Season to taste and serve over spaghetti. Serves 4.

## POMODORO

**1** Take 500 g (1 lb) ripe tomatoes and score a small cross in the base of each. Place in a large heatproof bowl and cover with boiling water. Leave for 2 minutes.

**2** Drain the tomatoes and allow to cool slightly. Peel the skin away from the cross and discard. Cut the tomatoes in half and scoop out the seeds with a teaspoon. Roughly chop the tomato flesh.

**3** Heat 2 tablespoons oil in a large pan and add 1 large chopped onion. Cook over low heat for 15 minutes, stirring occasionally, until very soft. Add 2 crushed cloves of garlic and cook for a further 2 minutes.

**4** Add the tomato flesh, 2 teaspoons sugar and salt and pepper to taste. Cook uncovered over a low heat for 20 minutes, stirring occasionally. Cool slightly and purée in a blender or food processor. Reheat and serve with penne. Serves 4.

## CARBONARA

**1** Remove and discard the rind from 8 rashers of bacon. Cut the bacon into thin strips. Place in a frying pan and cook over medium heat until brown and crisp.

**2** Cook 500 g (1 lb) of spaghetti in a large pan of boiling water until tender. Drain well in a colander and then return to the pan.

**3** Beat 4 eggs, 1 1/4 cups (315 ml/10 fl oz) cream and 1/2 cup (50 g/1 2/3 oz) freshly grated Parmesan cheese together. Add the bacon to the pasta and pour in the egg mixture.

**4** Toss well to combine the ingredients. Return to very low heat and toss for about 30 seconds–1 minute, until the sauce has cooked and slightly thickened. Serve immediately. Serves 4.

## PESTO

**1** Place 1/4 cup (40 g/1 1/3 oz) pine nuts in a frying pan, and cook, stirring, over low heat for a couple of minutes until golden. Transfer to a plate to cool.

**2** Put 2 firmly packed cups (100 g/3 1/3 oz) whole fresh basil leaves into a food processor. Crush 2 cloves of garlic and add to the basil.

**3** Finely grate 25 g (3/4 oz) Parmesan cheese and add to the processor along with the toasted pine nuts. Process until finely chopped.

**4** With the motor running, add 1/2 cup (125 ml/4 fl oz) extra virgin olive oil in a slow stream. Process until all the oil has been added and the mixture is a thick, slightly runny paste. Serve over fettucine. Serves 4.

# CLASSIC PASTA SAUCES

### PUTTANESCA

**1** Heat 2 tablespoons oil in a large pan, add 3 anchovy fillets and cook, stirring, for a couple of minutes, until the anchovies break up.

**2** Add 3 crushed cloves of garlic and 1/2 teaspoon chilli flakes to the pan. Stir-fry for a further minute, taking care not to burn the garlic or it will become bitter.

**3** Add two 425 g (13 1/2 oz) cans crushed tomatoes and bring to the boil. Reduce the heat to simmer, uncovered, for 20 minutes, or until the sauce has reduced and thickened.

**4** Stir in 2 tablespoons capers, 1/4 cup (35 g/1 1/4 oz) chopped black olives and 2 teaspoons chopped fresh oregano leaves. Cook for a further 10 minutes. Serve over spaghetti. Serves 4.

### BOSCAIOLA

**1** Wipe 500 g (1 lb) button mushrooms with a damp paper towel to remove any dirt. Slice the mushrooms finely, stems included.

**2** Heat 2 tablespoons oil in a large pan; add 1 chopped onion. Cook over medium heat for about 5 minutes, or until golden. Add 2 crushed cloves of garlic and cook for 1 minute further.

**3** Add the mushrooms and 425 g (13 1/2 oz) can crushed tomatoes to the pan; bring to the boil. Reduce the heat, cover and leave to simmer for 15 minutes.

**4** Stir in 2 tablespoons chopped flat-leaf parsley. Toss a little sauce through 500 g (1 lb) cooked fusilli and serve topped with the remaining sauce. Serves 4.

## AMATRICIANA

**1** Take 500 g (1 lb) ripe tomatoes and score a small cross in the base of each. Place in a large heatproof bowl and cover with boiling water. Leave for 2 minutes.

**2** Drain the tomatoes and allow to cool slightly. Peel the skin away from the cross and discard. Roughly chop the tomato flesh.

**3** Heat 30 g (1 oz) butter in a large frying pan, add a finely chopped onion and cook for 5 minutes over medium low heat, until soft and golden. Cut 6 thin slices of pancetta into small strips, and add to the onion. Cook for 2 minutes to brown.

**4** Add the tomatoes to the pan, along with 2 teaspoons of very finely chopped red chilli. Bring to the boil, reduce the heat and simmer uncovered for 20 minutes, stirring occasionally. Serve on bucatini. Serves 4.

## PRIMAVERA

**1** Trim the ends from 155 g (5 oz) of asparagus spears and cut into 1 cm (1/2 inch) lengths. Place in a heatproof bowl and cover with boiling water. Leave for 1 minute, drain and cool.

**2** Melt 40 g (1 1/3 oz) butter in a large pan, add 1 small onion, 1 small zucchini and 1 small carrot, all diced, and cook over moderate heat for about 7 minutes, until soft, stirring occasionally.

**3** Add the asparagus to the pan, and cook for 1 minute. Add 1/2 cup (125 ml/4 fl oz) cream, stir and then warm through. Season with salt and pepper to taste.

**4** Add 500 g (1 lb) cooked fettucine to the vegetable mixture with 30 g (1 oz) grated Parmesan cheese. Toss together, then serve immediately. Serves 4.

# PASTA AND PIZZA

## SUN-DRIED TOMATO AND SALAMI PIZZA

Preparation time: 40 minutes
Total cooking time: 35–45 minutes
Serves 4

1 green capsicum
1 red or yellow capsicum
1 cup (125 g/4 oz) grated
   Cheddar cheese
100 g (3¹/3 oz) salami, sliced
1 red onion, thinly sliced into
   rings
¹/2 cup (90 g/3 oz) black olives,
   pitted and sliced
150 g (4³/4 oz) bocconcini

*Pizza Base*
7 g (¹/4 oz) sachet dried yeast
¹/2 teaspoon salt
¹/2 teaspoon sugar
2¹/2 cups (250 g/8 oz) plain flour
1 cup (160 g/5¹/4 oz) sun-dried
   tomatoes, finely chopped
¹/2 cup (80 g/2²/3 oz) pine nuts,
   finely chopped

**1** Cut the capsicums into large flat pieces; remove the membrane and seeds. Place, skin-side-up, under a hot grill and cook until the skin blackens and blisters. Cool under a tea towel. Peel away the skin and cut the flesh into thin strips. Set aside.

**2 To make Pizza Base:** Mix the yeast, salt, sugar and 1 cup (250 ml/ 8 fl oz) warm water in a small bowl. Cover with plastic wrap and leave in a warm place for 10 minutes, until foamy. Sift the flour into a bowl, make a well in the centre and add the yeast mixture, sun-dried tomatoes and pine nuts. Mix to a dough.

**3** Preheat the oven to moderately hot 200°C (400°F/Gas 6). Knead the dough on a lightly floured surface for about 10 minutes, or until smooth and elastic. Roll out to a 35 cm (14 inch) round. Place on a 30 cm (12 inch) non-stick pizza tray, folding the edge over to form a rim.

**4** Sprinkle the pizza base with grated cheese. Top with salami, red onion, olives and roasted capsicum. Bake for 30–40 minutes, or until the base is cooked. Top with thinly sliced bocconcini and bake for a further 5 minutes, or until just melted.

### COOK'S FILE

**Variation:** Use sun-dried capsicum instead of tomato in the pizza base.

*Leave the yeast mixture in a warm place until it becomes foamy.*

*Top the base with grated cheese, onion, salami, olives and roasted capsicum.*

## CREAMY SEAFOOD RAVIOLI

Preparation time: 45 minutes +
  30 minutes standing
Total cooking time: 15 minutes
Serves 4

### Pasta
2 cups (250 g/8 oz) plain flour
pinch of salt
3 eggs
1 tablespoon olive oil
1 egg yolk, extra

### Filling
50 g (1²/₃ oz) butter, softened
3 cloves garlic, finely chopped
2 tablespoons finely chopped
  flat-leaf parsley
100 g (3¹/₃ oz) scallops, cleaned
  and finely chopped
100 g (3¹/₃ oz) raw prawn meat,
  finely chopped

### Sauce
3 tablespoons butter
3 tablespoons plain flour
1¹/₂ cups (375 ml/12 fl oz) milk
300 ml (9¹/₂ fl oz) cream
¹/₂ cup (125 ml/4 fl oz) white
  wine
¹/₂ cup (50 g/1²/₃ oz) grated
  Parmesan
2 tablespoons chopped flat-leaf
  parsley

**1 To make Pasta:** Sift the flour and salt into a bowl and make a well in the centre. Whisk the eggs, oil and 1 tablespoon water in a jug, then add gradually to the flour and mix to a firm dough. Gather into a ball.
**2** Knead on a lightly floured surface for 5 minutes, or until smooth and elastic. Place in a lightly oiled bowl, cover with plastic wrap and set aside for 30 minutes.
**3 To make Filling:** Mix together the butter, garlic, parsley, scallops and prawns. Set aside.
**4** Roll out a quarter of the pasta dough at a time until very thin (each portion of dough should be roughly 10 cm/4 inches wide when rolled). Place 1 teaspoonful of filling at 5 cm (2 inch) intervals down one side of each strip. Whisk the extra egg yolk with 3 tablespoons water. Brush along one side of the dough and between the filling. Fold the dough over the filling to meet the other side. Repeat with the remaining filling and dough. Press the edges of the dough together firmly to seal.
**5** Cut between the mounds with a knife or a fluted pastry cutter. Cook in batches in a large pan of rapidly boiling water for 6 minutes each batch (while the pasta is cooking make the sauce). Drain well and return to the pan to keep warm.
**6 To make Sauce:** Melt the butter in a pan, add the flour and cook over low heat for 2 minutes. Remove from the heat and gradually stir in the combined milk, cream and white wine. Cook over low heat until the sauce begins to thicken, stirring constantly to prevent lumps forming. Bring to the boil and simmer gently for 5 minutes. Add the Parmesan cheese and parsley and stir until combined. Remove from the heat, add to the ravioli and toss well.

### COOK'S FILE

**Note:** We set the pasta dough aside for 30 minutes to let the gluten in the flour relax. If you don't do this, you run the risk of making tough pasta.

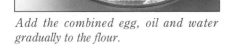

*Add the combined egg, oil and water gradually to the flour.*

*Knead on a lightly floured surface until smooth and elastic.*

*Mix together the butter, garlic, parsley, scallops and prawns.*

*Place a teaspoon of filling at intervals down one side of the pasta.*

*Cut between each mound of filling with a sharp knife.*

*Gradually stir in the combined milk, cream and white wine.*

## ROASTED TOMATO AND EGGPLANT PIZZA

Preparation time: 40 minutes
Total cooking time: 1 hour 45 minutes
Serves 4

500 g (1 lb) plum tomatoes
1 large eggplant
olive oil, for frying
200 g (6¹/2 oz) mozzarella,
    grated
¹/4 cup (25 g/³/4 oz) grated
    Parmesan
1 tablespoon chopped fresh
    oregano

*Pizza Base*
1 teaspoon dried yeast
¹/4 teaspoon salt
¹/4 teaspoon sugar
1¹/4 cups (155 g/5 oz) plain flour
6 cloves garlic, crushed

**1** Preheat the oven to slow 150°C (300°F/Gas 2). Cut the tomatoes in half and place in one layer on a baking tray, cut-side-up. Sprinkle with salt and roast for 1 hour 15 minutes. Set aside to cool.

**2 To make Pizza Base:** Put the yeast, salt, sugar and ¹/2 cup (125 ml/ 4 fl oz) warm water in a small bowl. Leave, covered with plastic wrap, in a warm place for 10 minutes, or until foamy. Sift the flour into a large bowl, make a well in the centre and add the yeast mixture and garlic. Mix to form a dough. Knead on a lightly floured surface for 10 minutes, or until smooth and elastic. Roll out to fit a 30 cm (12 inch) greased or non-stick pizza tray.

**3** Preheat the oven to moderately hot 200°C (400°F/Gas 6). Thinly slice the eggplant. Drizzle a char-grill or large frying pan with olive oil until nearly smoking. Add the eggplant in batches and cook, turning once, until soft (brush the eggplant with a little more oil if it starts to stick). Drain on paper towels.

**4** Arrange the eggplant on the pizza base. Top with tomatoes and sprinkle with the combined mozzarella and Parmesan. Bake for 20–30 minutes, or until the base is cooked and the cheese melted and golden. Sprinkle with fresh oregano to serve.

*Cut the tomatoes in half and sprinkle with sea salt.*

*Make a well in the centre of the flour and add the yeast and garlic.*

*Cook the eggplant in batches, turning once until soft.*

*Put the eggplant on the pizza base and top with the tomatoes.*

## SPAGHETTI WITH CHICKEN MEATBALLS

Preparation time: 30 minutes + chilling
Total cooking time: 1 hour 30 minutes
Serves 4–6

500 g (1 lb) chicken mince
60 g (2 oz) freshly grated
    Parmesan
2 cups (160 g/5¼ oz) fresh
    white breadcrumbs
2 cloves garlic, crushed
1 egg
freshly ground black pepper
1 tablespoon chopped fresh
    flat-leaf parsley
1 tablespoon chopped fresh sage
3 tablespoons vegetable oil

*Tomato Sauce*
1 tablespoon olive oil
1 onion, finely chopped
2 kg (4 lb) ripe tomatoes,
    coarsely chopped
2 bay leaves
1 cup (30 g/1 oz) fresh basil
    leaves, loosely packed
1 teaspoon coarse ground black
    pepper

500 g (1 lb) spaghetti
2 tablespoons chopped fresh
    oregano, to serve

**1** In a large bowl, mix together the mince, Parmesan, breadcrumbs, garlic, egg, pepper and herbs. Shape tablespoonsful of mixture into small balls and chill for 30 minutes to firm.

Heat the oil in a shallow pan and fry the balls in batches until golden brown; turn often by shaking the pan. Drain on paper towels.

**2 To make Tomato Sauce:** Heat the oil in a large pan, add the onion and fry for 1–2 minutes. Add the tomato and bay leaves, cover and bring to the boil, stirring occasionally. Reduce the heat to low, partially cover and cook for 50–60 minutes.

**3** Add the meatballs, basil leaves and pepper and simmer for 10–15 minutes, uncovered. Cook the spaghetti in boiling water until just tender. Drain; return to the pan. Add some sauce to the pasta and toss. Serve the pasta in individual bowls with sauce and meatballs, sprinkled with fresh oregano and perhaps extra Parmesan.

*Shape tablespoonsful of the mixture into small balls.*

*Partially cover the pan and cook for 50–60 minutes.*

*Add the meatballs, basil and pepper to the tomato mixture.*

## RICOTTA LASAGNE

Preparation time: 1 hour
Total cooking time: 1 hour 30 minutes
Serves 8

500 g (1 lb) fresh spinach
    lasagne sheets
1/2 cup (30 g/1 oz) fresh basil
    leaves, coarsely chopped
2 tablespoons fresh
    breadcrumbs
3 tablespoons pine nuts
2 teaspoons paprika
1 tablespoon grated Parmesan

*Ricotta Filling*
750 g (1 1/2 lb) fresh ricotta
1/2 cup (50 g/1 2/3 oz) grated
    Parmesan
freshly ground black pepper
pinch of nutmeg

*Tomato Sauce*
1 tablespoon olive oil
2 onions, chopped
2 cloves garlic, crushed
800 g (1 lb 10 oz) can crushed
    tomatoes
1 tablespoon tomato paste

*Béchamel Sauce*
60 g (2 oz) butter
1/2 cup (60 g/2 oz) plain flour
2 cups (500 ml/16 fl oz) milk
2 eggs, lightly beaten
1/3 cup (35 g/1 1/4 oz) grated
    Parmesan

**1** Lightly grease a 25 x 32 cm (10 x 13 inch) baking dish. Cut the pasta sheets into large pieces and cook, 2–3 at a time, in boiling water for 3 minutes. Drain and spread on damp tea towels until needed.

**2 To make Ricotta Filling:** Put the ricotta and Parmesan cheeses, pepper and nutmeg in a bowl and mix together well. Set aside.

**3 To make Tomato Sauce:** Heat the oil in a frying pan, add the onion and cook for about 10 minutes, stirring occasionally, until very soft. Add the garlic and cook for 1 more minute. Add the tomato and tomato paste and stir until well combined. Stir until the mixture comes to the boil. Reduce the heat and simmer uncovered for 15 minutes, or until thickened, stirring occasionally.

**4 To make Béchamel Sauce:** Heat the butter in a small pan. When starting to foam, add the flour and stir for 3 minutes, or until just coloured. Remove from the heat; add the milk gradually, stirring after each addition, then return to the heat and stir until sauce boils and thickens. Remove from the heat and stir in the eggs. Return to moderate heat and stir until almost boiling, but do not boil. Add the cheese and season to taste. Put plastic wrap onto the surface to prevent a skin forming. Preheat the oven to 200°C (400°F/Gas 6).

**5** Put a layer of lasagne sheets in the dish. Spread with a third of the Ricotta Filling, sprinkle with basil, then top with a third of the Tomato Sauce. Repeat the layers, finishing with pasta.

**6** Pour over the Béchamel Sauce, spread until smooth, then sprinkle with the combined breadcrumbs, pine nuts, paprika and Parmesan. Bake for 45 minutes, or until browned. Leave for 10 minutes before serving.

### COOK'S FILE

**Note:** Leaving the Lasagne to stand before serving makes it easier to cut.

*Cook the lasagne in a large pan of boiling water, 2–3 sheets at a time.*

*Simmer the Tomato Sauce, uncovered, for 15 minutes until it has thickened.*

*Stir the Béchamel Sauce until it boils and thickens.*

*Placing plastic wrap onto the surface of the sauce will stop a skin forming.*

*Use the back of a spoon to spread a layer of Tomato Sauce over the Ricotta Filling.*

*Sprinkle the pine nut and breadcrumb mixture over the Béchamel Sauce.*

35

# Pizzettas

### SUN-DRIED TOMATO PESTO AND ARTICHOKE

Preheat the oven to moderately hot 200°C (400°F/Gas 6). To make pesto, place 1/2 cup (75 g/2 1/2 oz) whole sun-dried tomatoes, 2 tablespoons pine nuts, 2 cloves of garlic and 2 tablespoons grated Parmesan cheese in a food processor. Process until smooth. Divide the pesto among 4 individual pizza bases. Slice 4 marinated artichoke hearts and place on top of the pesto. Sprinkle with 1 cup (150 g/4 3/4 oz) grated mozzarella cheese. Bake for 15–20 minutes, or until the base is crisp and the cheese has melted. Serves 4.

### BOCCONCINI AND TOMATO

Preheat the oven to moderately hot 200°C (400°F/Gas 6). Combine 3 tablespoons olive oil with 8 crushed cloves of garlic. Drizzle the mixture over 4 individual pizza bases. Bake for 10 minutes. Slice 4 egg tomatoes and place on the pizza bases. Top with 4 sliced fresh bocconcini, cracked black pepper and salt. Return to the oven and cook for a further 6 minutes, or until the cheese has melted. Sprinkle pizzettas with 1/2 cup (30 g/1 oz) shredded basil. Serves 4.

### CHAR-GRILLED CAPSICUM AND PROSCIUTTO

Preheat the oven to moderately hot 200°C (400°F/Gas 6). Spread 1 cup (250 g/8 oz) ready-made pizza sauce over 4 individual pizza bases. Cut 1 red and 1 green capsicum into large, flattish pieces and place, skin-side-up, under a hot grill. Cook until the skin blackens and blisters. Remove from the heat and cover with a tea towel; leave to cool. Peel away the skin and cut the flesh into thin strips. Divide among the pizza bases. Cut 12 thin slices of prosciutto into strips and place on top of the capsicum. Top the prosciutto with 2/3 cup (125 g/4 oz) good-quality black olives, pitted and sliced. Drizzle with extra virgin olive oil. Bake for 10–15 minutes, or until the crusts are golden. Serves 4.

## SWEET POTATO AND SCALLOP

Preheat the oven to moderately hot 200°C (400°F/Gas 6). Drizzle 4 individual pizza bases with olive oil. Clean and cut in half 250 g (8 oz) scallops and arrange on the bases. Very thinly slice 375 g (12 oz) sweet potato and deep-fry until golden and crisp; drain well. Thinly slice 1 red onion. Top the scallops with sweet potato and onion and drizzle with extra virgin olive oil. Bake for 10–15 minutes. Sprinkle with 2 tablespoons chopped fresh thyme to serve. Serves 4.

## HERBED TOMATO AND ROCKET

Preheat the oven to moderately hot 200°C (400°F/Gas 6). Heat 1 tablespoon olive oil in a pan. Add 1 finely chopped onion and 2 crushed cloves of garlic and cook over medium heat for 3–4 minutes. Peel and chop 500 g (1 lb) ripe egg tomatoes and add to the pan with 2 tablespoons chopped fresh herbs. Cook over high heat for 5–7 minutes, or until the mixture is quite thick; spread over 4 individual pizza bases. Bake for 10–15 minutes, or until the bases are crisp. Remove from the oven and top with 2 cups (40 g/1¹/₃ oz) torn rocket leaves. Sprinkle with shavings of Parmesan and season with cracked black pepper. Serves 4.

## CARAMELISED ONION AND GOATS CHEESE

Preheat the oven to moderately hot 200°C (400°F/Gas 6). Slice 4 onions very finely. Heat 2 tablespoons olive oil in a large pan; cook the onion over high heat for 2–3 minutes, or until starting to brown. Reduce the heat and cook for 15 minutes, or until the onion is soft. Spread the onion over 4 individual pizza bases. Top with 125 g (4 oz) goats cheese, crumbled or thinly sliced. Bake for 10–15 minutes, or until the crusts are golden. Remove from the oven and sprinkle with 2 tablespoons chopped fresh oregano. Serves 4.

*Pizzettas from left: Sun-dried Tomato Pesto and Artichoke; Bocconcini and Tomato; Char-grilled Capsicum and Prosciutto; Sweet Potato and Scallop; Herbed Tomato and Rocket; Caramelised Onion and Goats Cheese*

## POTATO ONION PIZZA

Preparation time: 40 minutes
Total cooking time: 40 minutes
Serves 4

7 g (¹/₄ oz) sachet dry yeast
¹/₂ teaspoon sugar
1¹/₂ cups (185 g/6 oz) plain flour
1 cup (150 g/4³/₄ oz) wholemeal
   plain flour
1 tablespoon olive oil

*Topping*
1 large red capsicum
1 potato, peeled
1 large onion, sliced
125 g (4 oz) soft goats cheese,
   crumbled

3 tablespoons capers
1 tablespoon dried oregano
1 teaspoon cracked pepper
1 teaspoon olive oil

**1** Mix the yeast, sugar, a good pinch of salt and 1 cup (250 ml/8 fl oz) warm water in a bowl. Cover with plastic wrap and leave in a warm place for 10 minutes, or until foamy. Sift both flours into a bowl. Make a well in the centre, add the yeast mixture and mix to a firm dough. Knead on a lightly floured surface for 5 minutes, or until smooth. Roll out to a 35 cm (14 inch) round. Brush a 30 cm (12 inch) pizza tray with oil; put the dough on the tray and tuck the edge over to form a rim. Preheat the oven to moderately hot 200°C (400°F/Gas 6).

**2** To make Topping: Cut the capsicum into large flat pieces; remove the seeds. Place, skin-side-up, under a hot grill until blackened. Cool under a tea towel, peel away the skin and cut the flesh into narrow strips.
**3** Slice the potato paper thin and arrange over the base with the onion, capsicum and half the goats cheese. Sprinkle with capers, oregano and pepper and drizzle with olive oil. Brush the edge of the crust with oil and bake for 20 minutes. Add the remaining goats cheese and bake for 15–20 minutes, or until the crust has browned. Cut into wedges to serve.

### COOK'S FILE

**Note:** Goats cheese, also known as Chèvre, is available at delicatessens.

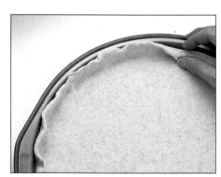

*Tuck the edge of the pizza dough over to form a rim.*

*Remove the skin from the capsicum and cut the flesh into thin strips.*

*Arrange the onion, capsicum and half the goats cheese over the base.*

## HAM AND CHEESE CALZONI

Preparation time: 30 minutes + chilling
Total cooking time: 30 minutes
Makes 4

2 cups (250 g/8 oz) plain flour
100 g (3¹/3 oz) butter, chopped
2 egg yolks

*Ham and Cheese Filling*
250 g (8 oz) ricotta cheese
50 g (1²/3 oz) Gruyère cheese, cubed
50 g (1²/3 oz) ham, finely chopped

2 spring onions, chopped
1 tablespoon chopped fresh flat-leaf parsley
freshly ground black pepper

**1** Lightly grease a large oven tray. Sift the flour and a pinch of salt into a bowl and rub in the butter. Make a well in the centre, cut in the egg yolks with a knife and add 2–3 tablespoons water, or enough to form a dough. Gather together into a ball, cover with plastic wrap and chill for 20 minutes. Preheat the oven to moderately hot 200°C (400°F/Gas 6).
**2 To make Filling:** Combine the cheeses, ham, spring onions, parsley and black pepper in a bowl.

**3** Roll out a quarter of the dough to make a large round 2–3 mm (1/8 inch) thick, trimming any uneven edges. Spoon a quarter of the filling mixture into the centre, brush the edge very lightly with water and fold over to enclose the filling, pressing the edge to seal. Repeat with the remaining dough and filling. Place the Calzoni on the oven tray, brush with a little olive oil and bake for 30 minutes, or until well browned and crisp.

### COOK'S FILE

**Note:** Calzoni can be made 1 day ahead and kept refrigerated before baking. Pastry can be made in a food processor, in short bursts.

*Use a knife to cut the egg yolks into the flour and butter mixture.*

*Mix together the cheeses, ham, spring onions, parsley and pepper in a bowl.*

*Brush the edge of the pastry with water, then fold over to enclose the filling.*

39

## CHICKEN TORTELLINI WITH TOMATO SAUCE

Preparation time: 30 minutes
+ resting
Total cooking time: 30 minutes
Serves 4

*Pasta*
2 cups (250 g/8 oz) plain flour
pinch of salt
3 eggs
1 tablespoon olive oil

*Filling*
20 g ($^2$/3 oz) butter
80 g (2$^2$/3 oz) chicken breast
    fillet, cubed
2 slices pancetta, chopped
$^1$/2 cup (50 g/1$^2$/3 oz) grated
    Parmesan
$^1$/2 teaspoon nutmeg
1 egg, lightly beaten

*Tomato Sauce*
$^1$/3 cup (80 ml/2$^3$/4 fl oz) olive oil
1$^1$/2 kg (3 lb) fresh ripe
    tomatoes, peeled and
    chopped
$^1$/4 cup (7 g/$^1$/4 oz) chopped fresh
    oregano
$^1$/2 cup (50 g/1$^2$/3 oz) grated
    Parmesan

100 g (3$^1$/3 oz) fresh bocconcini,
    thinly sliced, to serve

**1 To make Pasta:** Sift the flour
and salt into a bowl and make a well
in the centre. In a jug, whisk together
the eggs, oil and 1 tablespoon water.
Add the egg mixture gradually to the
flour, mixing to a firm dough. Gather
together into a ball, adding a little
extra water if necessary.

**2** Knead on a lightly floured surface
for 5 minutes, or until the dough is
smooth and elastic. Place in a lightly
oiled bowl, cover with plastic wrap
and leave for 30 minutes.

**3 To make Filling:** Heat the butter
in a frying pan; add the chicken and
cook until golden brown, then drain.
Process the chicken and pancetta in a
food processor or mincer until finely
chopped. Transfer to a bowl and add
the cheese, nutmeg, egg and salt and
pepper to taste. Set aside.

**4** Roll out the dough very thinly on a
lightly floured surface. Using a
floured cutter, cut into 5 cm (2 inch)
rounds. Spoon about $^1$/2 teaspoon of
filling into the centre of each round.
Fold the rounds in half to form semi-
circles, pressing the edges together
firmly. Wrap each semi-circle around
your finger to form a ring and then
press the ends of the dough together
firmly.

**5 To make Tomato Sauce:** Place
the oil, tomatoes and oregano in a frying pan and cook over high heat for
10 minutes. Stir through the Parmesan
cheese, then set aside.

**6** Cook the tortellini in two batches in
a large pan of rapidly boiling water
for about 6 minutes each batch, or
until just tender. Drain well and
return to the pan. Reheat the Tomato
Sauce, add to the tortellini and toss to
combine. Divide the tortellini among
individual bowls, top with bocconcini
and allow the cheese to melt a little
before serving.

### COOK'S FILE

**Hint:** To peel fresh tomatoes, score a
cross in the base of the tomato, put in
a bowl of boiling water for 1 minute,
then plunge into cold water. The skin
will peel away from the cross.

*Gather together the dough into a ball
with your hand.*

*Place the dough in a lightly oiled bowl,
cover with plastic wrap and leave.*

*Add the cheese, nutmeg, egg and season-
ing to the processed filling mixture.*

Roll out the dough very thinly and cut into rounds with a floured pastry cutter.

Wrap the semi-circles around your finger to make a ring. Press the ends together.

Stir the grated Parmesan into the Tomato Sauce.

# VEGETABLE DISHES

## EGGPLANT PARMIGIANA

Preparation time: 30 minutes
Total cooking time: 1 hour 15 minutes
Serves 6–8

3 tablespoons olive oil
1 onion, diced
2 cloves garlic, crushed
1.25 kg (2 lb 8 oz) tomatoes,
    peeled and chopped
1 kg (2 lb) eggplants
250 g (8 oz) bocconcini, sliced
185 g (6 oz) Cheddar cheese,
    finely grated
1 cup (50 g/1²/3 oz) basil leaves
¹/2 cup (50 g/1²/3 oz) grated
    Parmesan

**1** Heat the oil in a large frying pan; add the onion and cook over moderate heat until soft. Add the garlic and cook for 1 minute. Add the tomato and simmer for 15 minutes. Season with salt to taste. Preheat the oven to moderately hot 200°C (400°F/Gas 6).

**2** Slice the eggplants very thinly and shallow-fry in oil in batches for 3–4 minutes, or until golden brown. Drain on paper towels.

**3** Place one third of the eggplant in a 7-cup (1.75 litre) ovenproof dish. Top with half the bocconcini and Cheddar. Repeat the layers, finishing with a layer of eggplant.

**4** Pour over the tomato mixture. Scatter with torn basil leaves, then Parmesan. Bake for 40 minutes.

*Fry the onion and garlic in the oil, then add the chopped tomato.*

*Shallow-fry the eggplant in batches, then drain on paper towels.*

*Arrange layers of eggplant, bocconcini and Cheddar in the dish.*

*Pour over the tomato sauce and sprinkle with torn basil leaves and Parmesan.*

## STUFFED ZUCCHINI

Preparation time: 20 minutes
Total cooking time: 45 minutes
Serves 4

8 zucchini
35 g (1¼ oz) white bread,
 crusts removed
milk, for soaking
125 g (4 oz) ricotta cheese
3 tablespoons grated Cheddar
 cheese

⅓ cup (35 g/1¼ oz) grated
 Parmesan
2 teaspoons chopped fresh
 oregano
2 teaspoons chopped fresh
 thyme
1 clove garlic, crushed
1 egg yolk

**1** Preheat the oven to moderately hot 190°C (375°F/Gas 5). Cook the zucchini in boiling salted water for 5 minutes, then drain. Meanwhile, soak the bread in milk until soft, then squeeze dry.

Cut the zucchini in half and scoop out the flesh with a teaspoon.

**2** Chop the zucchini flesh finely. Place in a bowl and add the bread, cheeses, herbs, garlic, egg yolk and season with salt and pepper. Mix together, adding a little milk to make it bind together if necessary.

**3** Fill the zucchini shells with the stuffing. Brush an ovenproof baking dish with oil and arrange the zucchini close together. Bake in the oven for 35–40 minutes, until golden on top. Serve immediately.

*Cut the zucchini in half and scoop out the flesh with a teaspoon.*

*Combine the zucchini, cheeses, herbs, garlic and egg yolk in a bowl.*

*Arrange the stuffed zucchini close together in the oiled baking dish.*

*Fry the onion in the butter and then add the garlic and pancetta.*

*Add a little stock from time to time as the liquid is absorbed.*

*When cooled a little, stir through the eggs, Parmesan and pepper.*

*Lightly grease a springform tin and then sprinkle with dry breadcrumbs.*

## SPINACH AND PANCETTA PIE

Preparation time: 30 minutes
Total cooking time: 55 minutes
Serves 4–6

45 g (1¹/2 oz) butter
2 tablespoons olive oil
1 large onion, finely chopped
2 cloves garlic, finely chopped
125 g (4 oz) finely sliced
    pancetta, chopped
1 cup (220 g/7 oz) arborio rice
3 cups (750 ml/24 fl oz) beef
    stock
800 g (1 lb 10 oz) English
    spinach, coarsely chopped
4 eggs, lightly beaten
¹/2 cup (50 g/1²/3 oz) freshly
    grated Parmesan
1 teaspoon coarsely cracked
    black pepper
4 tablespoons dry breadcrumbs

**1** Heat the butter and 1 tablespoon oil in a large frying pan and cook the onion for 3–4 minutes. Add the garlic and pancetta and cook for 1 minute.
**2** Add the rice and stir to coat. Pour in half the stock, reduce the heat, cover and simmer for 8 minutes, adding the remaining stock gradually as it is absorbed. Continue cooking the rice until all the stock has been absorbed. Preheat the oven to moderate 180°C (350°F/Gas 4).
**3** Fold the spinach into the rice, cover and simmer for a further 2 minutes, or until just wilted. Transfer to a bowl and leave to cool a little. Stir in the eggs, Parmesan and cracked pepper.
**4** Sprinkle a greased 23 cm (9 inch) springform tin with 3 tablespoons of the breadcrumbs. Spoon in the filling, drizzle with the remaining oil and sprinkle the remaining breadcrumbs over the top. Bake for 40–45 minutes, then cool in the tin. Cut into wedges and serve at room temperature.

### COOK'S FILE

**Note:** Ready-made stock in a tetra pack is very good but can be salty: use half stock, half water.

## PEPPERONATA TART

Preparation time: 30 minutes + chilling
Total cooking time: 1 hour
Serves 4–6

2¹/2 cups (310 g/9³/4 oz) plain
    flour
pinch of cayenne pepper
125 g (4 oz) butter, cubed
90 g (3 oz) cream cheese, cubed
1 egg yolk, beaten
1 tablespoon lemon juice

*Filling*
1 large red capsicum
1 large green capsicum
2 large yellow capsicums
2 tablespoons olive oil
3 large onions, sliced into rings
400 g (12²/3 oz) can chopped
    tomatoes
fresh thyme leaves, to garnish

**1** Sift the flour, a pinch of salt and cayenne pepper into a food processor. Add the butter, cream cheese, combined egg yolk and lemon juice and process in short bursts, adding 2–3 tablespoons water, until the mixture forms a firm dough when pressed together. Turn onto a lightly floured surface and gather together into a ball. Wrap in plastic wrap and chill for 30 minutes. Roll out to fit a 25 cm (10 inch) greased springform tin, to cover the base and halfway up the side. Refrigerate for 30 minutes.

**2** Preheat the oven to moderately hot 200°C (400°F/Gas 6). Put baking paper over the pastry and fill with rice or dried beans. Bake for 15 minutes, then reduce the oven to moderate 180°C (350°F/Gas 4), remove the beans and paper and cook for 15–20 minutes, or until golden brown. Cool.

**3 To make Filling:** Cut capsicums into large pieces and de-seed. Place, skin-side-up, under a hot grill until black. Cool under a tea towel. Remove the skins and chop the flesh.

**4** Heat the oil and fry the onions for 3–4 minutes, or until soft. Add the tomatoes, capsicum and seasoning to taste. Cook, uncovered, over low heat for 10 minutes until the liquid has reduced. Cool, then spoon into the pastry case and sprinkle with fresh thyme to serve.

*Process until the mixture forms a firm dough when pressed together.*

*Cooling the capsicum under a tea towel makes the skin easier to peel away.*

*Use uncooked rice, chickpeas or beans for blind baking pastry.*

*Spoon the capsicum and tomato filling into the pastry base.*

## ROLLED CAPSICUMS

Preparation time: 20 minutes
  + 30 minutes marinating
Total cooking time: 10 minutes
Serves 6

2 large red capsicums
2 large yellow capsicums
2 large green capsicums
3 tablespoons olive oil
1 teaspoon lemon juice
2 cloves garlic, crushed

185 g (6 oz) flaked tuna, drained
100 g (3¹/3 oz) anchovies,
  drained and chopped
¹/3 cup (60 g/2 oz) black olives,
  pitted and chopped
2 tablespoons capers, drained
1 tablespoon chopped fresh
  parsley

**1** Cut the capsicums into quarters lengthways, remove the seeds and membrane and brush the skin with a little of the oil. Cook until a hot grill, skin-side-up, until the skins are black and blistered. Cover with a tea towel and leave to cool. Peel away the skin.

**2** Combine the remaining oil, lemon juice, garlic and a little salt. Marinate the capsicums in this for 30 minutes. In another bowl, mix together the tuna, anchovies, olives and capers.

**3** Drain the capsicums, reserving the marinade, and place 2 teaspoons of tuna filling on each piece. Roll up and arrange on a serving dish. Drizzle with the reserved marinade and then garnish with chopped parsley and cracked black pepper.

*Remove the seeds and membrane from the capsicums.*

*Leave the capsicum in the marinade for 30 minutes.*

*Place 2 teaspoonsful of filling on each piece of capsicum and roll up.*

## CAPONATA

Preparation time: 25 minutes
Total cooking time: 35 minutes
Serves 6

3 tablespoons olive oil
2 onions, sliced
2 red capsicums, thinly sliced
4 cloves garlic, finely chopped
4 celery sticks, sliced
1 large eggplant (500 g/1 lb), cubed
1 kg (2.2 lb) fresh tomatoes, peeled and chopped

2 tablespoons fresh thyme leaves
2 tablespoons sugar
1/2 cup (125 ml/4 fl oz) red wine vinegar
125 g (4 oz) pitted green olives, rinsed well and drained
2 tablespoons capers, drained

**1** Heat the oil in a large frying pan and add the onion, capsicum, garlic, celery and eggplant. Cover and then leave to simmer over low heat for 20 minutes. Season to taste with salt and freshly ground black pepper.
**2** Add the tomatoes and thyme and leave to simmer, uncovered, for a further 15 minutes.
**3** Add the sugar, vinegar, olives and capers to the vegetables and mix well. Taste and season again if necessary before serving. Serve warm or at room temperature.

### COOK'S FILE

**Hint:** Peel fresh tomatoes by scoring a cross in the top of the tomato and placing in a bowl of boiling water for 1 minute. Plunge into cold water and peel the skin away from the cross.
**Note:** Green olives are picked and processed when they are unripe.

*Thinly slice the capsicum, onion and celery. Finely chop the garlic.*

*Leave to simmer for 20 minutes, then season to taste with salt and pepper.*

*Add the sugar, vinegar, olives and capers to the pan and mix well.*

## ASPARAGUS WITH PARMESAN

Preparation time: 15 minutes
Total cooking time: 10 minutes
Serves 4

60 g (2 oz) butter
2 tablespoons grated fresh Parmesan
1/2 cup (40 g/1 1/3 oz) fresh breadcrumbs
2 tablespoons pine nuts, chopped

1 clove garlic, finely chopped
2 teaspoons chopped fresh oregano
2 teaspoons chopped fresh flat-leaf parsley
freshly ground black pepper
500 g (1 lb) fresh asparagus
60 g (2 oz) butter, melted, for serving

**1** Heat the butter in a pan and, when foaming, add the Parmesan cheese, breadcrumbs and pine nuts. Stir over medium heat until lightly browned and crisp, then add the garlic, herbs and pepper and mix well.
**2** Boil, steam or microwave the asparagus for 2–3 minutes, or until just tender, then rinse under cold water and pat dry with paper towels.
**3** Serve the asparagus immediately, sprinkled with the crisp Parmesan topping and drizzled with extra melted butter.

### COOK'S FILE

**Note:** Use slightly stale bread to make breadcrumbs in a processor.

*Chop the pine nuts, garlic, fresh oregano and flat-leaf parsley.*

*Brown the cheese, breadcrumbs and nuts then add the garlic, herbs and pepper.*

*It is easier to handle the asparagus if you keep them tied together during cooking.*

*Caponata (top) and Asparagus with Parmesan*

## BAKED MUSHROOMS

Preparation time: 15 minutes
Total cooking time: 15 minutes
Serves 4

250 g (8 oz) button mushrooms
200 g (6¹/2 oz) oyster mushrooms
200 g (6¹/2 oz) shiitake
 mushrooms
100 g (3¹/3 oz) Swiss brown
 mushrooms

*Topping*
1 cup (80 g/2²/3 oz) fresh
 breadcrumbs

¹/4 cup (25 g/³/4 oz) freshly
 grated Parmesan
2 tablespoons chopped fresh
 flat-leaf parsley
1 tablespoon chopped fresh
 thyme
2 cloves garlic, crushed
1 teaspoon cracked pepper
2 tablespoons extra virgin
 olive oil

**1** Preheat the oven to moderate 180°C (350°F/Gas 4). Wipe the mushrooms with damp paper towel. Trim away the hard tips and discard. Cut any large mushrooms in half lengthways.
**2** Sprinkle the base of a large baking

dish with a little water. Place the mushrooms in a single layer in the dish, stems upwards.
**3 To make Topping:** Mix together the breadcrumbs, Parmesan, herbs, garlic and pepper, sprinkle over the mushrooms and drizzle with oil. Bake for 12–15 minutes and serve warm.

### COOK'S FILE

**Note:** Use day-old bread which is slightly stale to make breadcrumbs. Simply remove the crusts and chop in a food processor until crumbs form.
**Hint:** Always wipe mushrooms clean with a damp paper towel—washing will make them soggy.

*Trim the hard tips from the stalks and cut any large mushrooms in half.*

*Place the mushrooms, stems upwards, in one layer in a baking dish.*

*Mix together the breadcrumbs, cheese, herbs, garlic and pepper.*

*Put the spinach, cheese, pepper and nutmeg in a bowl and mix well.*

*Cook until both sides of the pancake are golden, then remove with a spatula.*

*Remove from the heat and add salt and pepper, to taste, and grated cheese.*

*Divide the filling among the pancakes and roll up.*

## CHEESE AND SPINACH PANCAKES

Preparation time: 40 minutes
Total cooking time: 50 minutes
Serves 4

250 g (8 oz) cooked, drained
   English spinach, chopped
1/2 cup (125 g/4 oz) ricotta
   cheese
1/4 cup (30 g/1 oz) grated
   Cheddar cheese
ground black pepper
freshly grated nutmeg
1/4 cup (25 g/3/4 oz) grated
   Parmesan
1/2 teaspoon paprika
1/2 cup (40 g/1 1/3 oz) fresh
   breadcrumbs

*Batter*
1 cup (125 g/4 oz) plain flour
1 1/4 cups (315 ml/10 fl oz)
   milk
1 egg
butter, for cooking

*Cheese Sauce*
2 tablespoons butter
1/4 cup (30 g/1 oz) plain flour
1 3/4 cups (440 ml/14 fl oz) milk
1 cup (125 g/4 oz) grated
   Cheddar cheese

**1** Put the spinach, cheeses, pepper and nutmeg in a bowl and mix well.
**2 To make Batter:** Sift the flour and a pinch of salt into a bowl. Add half the milk and the egg. Whisk until smooth; add the remaining milk. Heat a teaspoon of butter in a frying pan and pour in a thin layer of batter. Cook the base until golden, then flip. The batter should make 8 pancakes.
**3 To make Cheese Sauce:** Melt the butter over low heat, add the flour and cook for 1 minute. Remove from the heat and slowly stir in the milk. Bring to the boil, stirring constantly. Remove from the heat and add salt and pepper and the grated cheese.
**4** Preheat the oven to 180°C (350°F/ Gas 4). Divide the filling among the pancakes, roll up and put in a greased ovenproof dish. Pour Cheese Sauce over the pancakes. Mix the Parmesan, paprika and breadcrumbs together and sprinkle over the sauce. Bake for 30 minutes, or until golden brown.

*Dissolve the sugar in the water, add the yeast and leave until frothy.*

*Cook the onions in the oil until they are soft and golden.*

*Knead the dough on a floured surface for about 10 minutes, until smooth.*

*Spread the cooked onion over the pizza base and then scatter with olives.*

## OLIVE AND ONION TART

Preparation time: 25 minutes
Total cooking time: 35–40 minutes
Serves 4–6

1 teaspoon sugar
1¹/₂ teaspoons dried yeast
¹/₂ cup (125 ml/4 fl oz) olive oil
5 onions, thinly sliced
1 cup (125 g/4 oz) self-raising
    flour
¹/₂ cup (125 g/4 oz) plain white
    flour
1 cup (185 g/6 oz) black olives
2 tablespoons grated Parmesan
    cheese

**1** Dissolve the sugar in ¹/₂ cup (125 ml/ 4 fl oz) warm water. Sprinkle with yeast and leave for 10 minutes, or until frothy.
**2** Heat 3 tablespoons oil in a frying pan and fry the onion for 10 minutes, or until soft. Leave to cool. Preheat the oven to hot 220°C (425°F/Gas 7).
**3** Sift together the self-raising flour, plain flour and a good pinch of salt in a bowl. Make a well in the centre and pour in the yeast mixture and 2 tablespoons oil. Bring together to form a dough and knead on a lightly floured surface for 10 minutes, or until smooth. Extra flour may be necessary.
**4** Roll out the dough to line a greased 30 cm (12 inch) pizza tray. Spread with cooked onions, then olives. Brush the crust with the remaining olive oil. Bake for 25–30 minutes. Serve hot or cold, sprinked with grated Parmesan.

## FENNEL WITH PECORINO CHEESE

Preparation time: 15 minutes
Total cooking time: 25 minutes
Serves 4

4 fennel bulbs
1 clove garlic, crushed
1/2 lemon, sliced
2 tablespoons olive oil
1 teaspoon salt
3 tablespoons butter, melted
2 tablespoons grated pecorino cheese

**1** Cut the top shoots and base off the fennel and remove the tough outer layers. Cut into segments and place in a pan with the garlic, lemon, oil and salt. Cover with water and bring to the boil. Reduce the heat and simmer for 20 minutes, or until just tender.

**2** Drain well and place in a heatproof dish. Drizzle with the butter. Sprinkle with the cheese and season with salt and pepper to taste.

**3** Place under a preheated grill until the cheese has browned. Best served immediately.

### COOK'S FILE

**Note:** If pecorino (a hard sheeps milk cheese) is not available, then use Parmesan instead.

*Trim the tops and bases from the fennel and remove the tough outer layers.*

*Place the fennel, garlic, lemon, oil and salt in a pan.*

*Sprinkle grated pecorino cheese over the fennel and brown under a grill.*

53

## MUSHROOMS IN TOMATO SAUCE

Preparation time: 15 minutes
Total cooking time: 20 minutes
Serves 4 as a side dish

2 tablespoons olive oil
2 cloves garlic, sliced
600 g (1¼ lb) large button
   mushrooms, halved

2 tablespoons tomato paste
2 tablespoons chopped fresh
   marjoram
250 g (8 oz) cherry tomatoes,
   halved
freshly ground black pepper
1 tablespoon chopped fresh
   oregano leaves

**1** Heat the oil in a pan, add the garlic and stir over moderate heat for 1 minute; do not brown.

**2** Add the mushrooms and cook, stirring, for 5 minutes, until combined and beginning to soften.
**3** Stir through the tomato paste, marjoram and cherry tomatoes and cook over low heat until the mushrooms are soft. Serve sprinkled with pepper and oregano leaves.

### COOK'S FILE

**Note:** Can be made up to two days ahead and served hot or cold.

*Stir the garlic over medium heat until fragrant but not browned.*

*Add the mushrooms to the pan and stir until they begin to soften.*

*Cook over low heat until the mushrooms are soft.*

Cook the leek until soft, then add the stock, thyme and potato.

Lift out half the potato with tongs and put into an ovenproof dish.

Spoon the leek and stock mixture around the side, trying to keep the top dry.

Bake, uncovered, until the potatoes on top are golden brown.

## OVEN-BAKED POTATO, LEEK AND OLIVES

Preparation time: 20 minutes
Total cooking time: 1 hour
Serves 4–6

2 tablespoons extra virgin
 olive oil
1 leek, finely sliced
1½ cups (375 ml/12 fl oz)
 chicken stock
2 teaspoons chopped fresh
 thyme
1 kg (2 lb) potatoes, unpeeled,
 cut into thin slices
6–8 pitted black olives, sliced
½ cup (50 g/1²/3 oz) freshly
 grated Parmesan
30 g (1 oz) butter, chopped

**1** Preheat the oven to moderate 180°C (350°F/Gas 4). Brush a shallow 5-cup (1.25 litre) ovenproof dish with a little olive oil. Heat the remaining oil in a large pan and cook the leek over moderate heat until soft. Add the stock, thyme and potato. Cover and leave to simmer for 5 minutes.
**2** Using tongs, lift out half the potato and put in the ovenproof dish. Sprinkle with olives and Parmesan and season with salt and pepper.
**3** Layer with the remaining potato, then spoon the leek and stock mixture in at the side of the dish, keeping the top dry.
**4** Scatter chopped butter over the potato and then bake, uncovered, for 50 minutes, or until cooked and golden brown. Leave in a warm place for about 10 minutes before serving.

### COOK'S FILE

**Note:** Keeping the top layer of potato dry as you pour in the stock mixture will give it a crisp finish.

# SEAFOOD

## TUNA STEAKS WITH WARM BEAN SALAD

Preparation time: 15 minutes
Total cooking time: 10 minutes
Serves 4

4 tuna steaks
olive oil, for brushing
finely shredded rind of 1 lemon

*Warm Bean Salad*
3 tablespoons olive oil
1 clove garlic, crushed
3 spring onions, chopped
1 small red capsicum, chopped
600 g (1¼ lb) can cannellini
    beans, rinsed and drained
1 radicchio, washed and
    separated into leaves
12 small black olives
1 tablespoon lemon juice

**1** Brush the tuna steaks with oil and cook in a frying pan (or ribbed pan or char-grill) for 2–3 minutes each side. (Tuna should be rare in the centre but you may prefer to cook it for another minute each side.) Transfer to a plate, cover loosely with foil and leave in a warm place for 5 minutes.
**2 To make Warm Bean Salad:** Heat the oil in a pan and cook the garlic, spring onions and capsicum until soft but not brown. Add the beans and radicchio and stir gently until the radicchio is wilted. Add the olives and lemon juice and season to taste with salt and pepper.
**3** Place the salad on individual plates, top with the tuna steaks and lemon rind. Serve immediately.

### COOK'S FILE

**Hint:** Use a lemon zester to make fine shreds of lemon rind.

Wash the radicchio and separate out into single leaves.

Tuna steaks should be rare in the middle, but you might prefer to cook them longer.

Transfer the tuna steaks to a plate and cover loosely with foil.

Add the beans and radicchio and stir gently until the leaves have wilted.

## WHITEBAIT FRITTERS

Preparation time: 20 minutes + resting
Total cooking time: 15 minutes
Makes 10

1/4 cup (30 g/1 oz) self-raising
   flour
1/4 cup (30 g/1 oz) plain flour
1/2 teaspoon bicarbonate of soda
1 teaspoon salt
freshly ground black pepper
1 egg, lightly beaten

3 tablespoons dry white wine
2 teaspoons chopped fresh
   flat-leaf parsley
1 clove garlic, crushed
1/2 small onion, grated
200 g (6 1/2 oz) Chinese or New
   Zealand whitebait
olive oil, for shallow frying
lemon wedges, to serve

**1** Sift the flours, bicarbonate of soda, salt and pepper into a bowl. Stir through the egg and wine, whisk until smooth, then add the parsley, garlic,

onion and whitebait. Cover and leave for 20 minutes.

**2** Heat the oil in a frying pan and then drop in tablespoons of batter. When the batter is puffed and bubbles appear on the surface, carefully turn to cook the other side.

**3** Drain on paper towels and serve immediately with lemon wedges.

### COOK'S FILE

**Note:** The Chinese or New Zealand whitebait is very small and fine and can be bought fresh or frozen.

*Add the parsley, garlic, onion and whitebait, cover and leave for 20 minutes.*

*Heat the oil in a frying pan, then drop in tablespoons of batter.*

*Cook both sides of the fritters, then lift out of the pan and drain on paper towels.*

*Remove the clear quills from inside the calamari and purple skin from outside.*

*Add the breadcrumbs, parsley and Parmesan and mix until well combined.*

*Divide the filling among the calamari tubes but don't fill them completely.*

*Shallow-fry the calamari in batches for 3–4 minutes on each side.*

## STUFFED CALAMARI

Preparation time: 30 minutes
Total cooking time: 20 minutes
Serves 4

8 medium calamari tubes
40 g (1¹/3 oz) butter
8 slices pancetta, finely chopped
400 g (12²/3 oz) raw prawns, peeled, deveined and finely chopped
1 cup (80 g/2²/3 oz) fresh breadcrumbs
¹/4 cup (10 g/¹/3 oz) chopped fresh parsley
1 cup (100 g/3¹/3 oz) grated Parmesan
100 g (3¹/3 oz) butter, extra
3 cloves garlic, crushed
1 tablespoon chopped fresh parsley, extra

**1** Rinse the calamari under cold water. Put your hand in and remove the insides and quill. Then remove the purple skin from the outside. Rinse and pat dry with paper towels.
**2** Melt the butter in a small frying pan; cook the pancetta and prawns over high heat until the prawns are just cooked. Transfer to a bowl; add the breadcrumbs, parsley and Parmesan and mix well.
**3** Divide the filling among the calamari tubes. Melt the extra butter with the garlic in a large frying pan and cook the stuffed calamari, in batches, for 3–4 minutes on each side, or until just cooked. Stir through the extra parsley. Place two stuffed calamari on each plate and spoon over a little of the garlic butter.

### COOK'S FILE

**Note:** You will only need to three-quarters-fill each calamari tube—the tubes shrink a little when cooked and if there is too much filling it will ooze out from the top.

## BAKED FISH WITH GARLIC BREADCRUMBS

Preparation time: 15 minutes
Total cooking time: 20 minutes
Serves 4

4 fillets firm white fish
    (about 200 g/6¹/2 oz each)
75 g (2¹/2 oz) butter, melted
3 cloves garlic, crushed
2 cups (160 g/5¹/4 oz) fresh
    white breadcrumbs
    (made from Italian bread)
1 tablespoon finely chopped
    parsley
lemon wedges, to serve

**1** Preheat the oven to moderately hot 200°C (400°F/Gas 6). Brush an ovenproof dish with olive oil and arrange the fish in a single layer.
**2** Mix together the butter and garlic in a bowl and set aside. Mix together the breadcrumbs and parsley and scatter in a thick layer over the fish. Drizzle with the garlic butter.
**3** Bake for 20 minutes, or until the fish is white and flakes easily and the crumbs are golden brown. If the crumbs are not golden but the fish is cooked, flash under a hot grill for a couple of minutes. Don't take your eyes off it as it can burn very quickly. Serve with lemon wedges.

**COOK'S FILE**

**Note:** Fresh breadcrumbs are very simple to make. Remove the crusts from slightly stale (at least one-day old) slices of bread. Put the bread in a food processor and mix until crumbs form. Use ordinary bread or, as in this recipe, Italian bread.

*Brush an ovenproof dish with olive oil and arrange the fish in a single layer.*

*Mix together the fresh breadcrumbs and parsley and scatter over the fish.*

*Bake until the fish is white and can be easily flaked with a fork.*

## FISH IN PARCHMENT

Preparation time: 20 minutes
Total cooking time: 20 minutes
Serves 4

4 deep sea perch fillets (about
    150–200 g/5–6 oz each)
1 leek, white part only, cut into
    julienne strips (see note)
4 spring onions, cut into julienne
    strips
2 teaspoons finely chopped
    chives, optional
30 g (1 oz) butter
1 lemon, cut into 12 very
    thin slices
juice of 1 lemon, extra

**1** Preheat the oven to moderate 180°C (350°F/Gas 4). Place each fish fillet in the centre of a piece of baking paper large enough to enclose the fish.
**2** Scatter over the leek, spring onion and chives. Top each with a teaspoon of butter and 3 slices of lemon. Squeeze over the extra lemon juice. Bring the top and bottom edges of the paper together and fold over, then scrunch over the sides to make a parcel. Put on a baking tray and bake for 20 minutes.
**3** Check to see that the fish is cooked (it should be white and easily flaked with a fork) and then serve. You can either let each person open their own parcel or take out the fish with an egg slice and serve on warm plates. Good with mixed wild and brown rice.

**COOK'S FILE**

**Note:** Julienne strips are thin, regular, matchstick-sized pieces of vegetables. They cook quickly and look attractive.

*Slice the leek and the spring onions very finely to make julienne strips.*

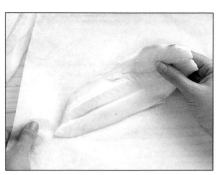

*Place each fish fillet in the centre of a piece of baking paper.*

*Scatter over the julienne vegetables and top with butter and lemon slices.*

*Baked Fish with Garlic Breadcrumbs (top) and*
*Fish in Parchment*

## BAKED TROUT WITH FENNEL AND WATER CHESTNUTS

Preparation time: 20 minutes
Total cooking time: 20–30 minutes
Serves 4

4 whole small trout, cleaned
and gutted

1 tablespoon sea salt
1 teaspoon cracked black
pepper
2 fennel bulbs, trimmed and
thinly sliced
230 g (7¹/₃ oz) canned water
chestnuts, drained
¹/₂ cup (125 ml/4 fl oz) fresh
lemon juice
¹/₂ cup (125 ml/4 fl oz) dry
white wine

**1** Preheat the oven to moderate 180°C (350°F/Gas 4). Arrange the trout, side by side, in a large baking dish, and sprinkle with sea salt and pepper.
**2** Top with the sliced fennel and water chestnuts. Pour over the lemon juice and wine and cover with foil.
**3** Bake for 20–30 minutes, or until the fish flakes with a fork and the fennel is tender, then remove the foil and serve immediately.

*Trim the stalk and base from the fennel bulbs and thinly slice.*

*Arrange the trout, side-by-side, in a dish and sprinkle with salt and pepper.*

*Top the trout with fennel and chestnuts, then pour over the lemon juice and wine.*

*Remove the head of the sardine, cut through the gut and open out flat.*

*Scrape the flesh away from the backbone, cut at either end and lift out the bone.*

*Mix together the breadcrumbs, garlic, capers, cheese, pepper and egg yolk.*

*Spoon a little stuffing onto each sardine, put on the oven tray and bake.*

## STUFFED SARDINES

Preparation time: 40 minutes
Total cooking time: 20 minutes
Serves 4

8 large sardines
1/3 cup (35 g/1¼ oz) dry
    breadcrumbs
1 clove garlic, crushed
1 tablespoon capers, finely
    chopped
2 tablespoons grated fresh
    Parmesan
freshly ground black pepper
1 egg yolk, lightly beaten
juice of 1 lemon, to serve

**1** Preheat the oven to moderately hot 200°C (400°F/Gas 6). Lightly grease an oven tray.
**2** Remove the heads from the sardines, make a slit through the gut and open out flat. Remove the guts and carefully scrape the flesh away from the backbone; trim at the tail end leaving the tail intact. Lift out the backbone; discard. Wash the sardines well and drain on paper towels.
**3** Mix together the breadcrumbs, garlic, capers, Parmesan, pepper and enough egg yolk to bind the stuffing together. Spoon a little onto each open sardine, put on the oven tray and bake for 20 minutes, until golden. Serve drizzled with lemon juice.

### COOK'S FILE

**Note:** You can buy sardines already filleted at some fishmongers. This makes the recipe quick and simple.

*Cut open the octopus heads and discard the guts.*

*Remove the beaks from the octopus and cut the tentacles into sections.*

*Toss the octopus over high heat until it becomes opaque.*

## OCTOPUS IN FRESH TOMATO SAUCE

Preparation time: 20 minutes
Total cooking time: 1 hour 10 minutes
Serves 4–6

1 kg (2 lb) baby octopus
2 tablespoons olive oil
1/3 cup (80 ml/2³/4 fl oz) dry
    white wine
500 g (1 lb) ripe tomatoes,
    peeled and chopped
4 pickling onions, peeled and
    quartered
1 clove garlic, chopped
2 tablespoons chopped fresh
    flat-leaf parsley

**1** Wash the octopus and cut the heads off. Cut open the heads and remove the guts. Wash the heads and drain. Remove the beaks and cut the tentacles into sets of four.
**2** Heat the oil in a large pan until very hot, add the octopus and toss over high heat for about 10 minutes, or until the octopus is opaque and the pan almost dry. Add the wine and simmer, uncovered, until most of the liquid has evaporated, then add the tomato and onions. Bring to the boil, then reduce the heat and simmer over low heat for 45 minutes to 1 hour, or until tender.
**3** Serve hot or warm, sprinkled with the combined chopped garlic and parsley and lots of black pepper.

*When most of the liquid has evaporated add the tomato and onions.*

### COOK'S FILE

**Note:** To peel tomatoes, cut a cross in the base, plunge in boiling water then into cold. Peel the skin from the cross.

## PAN-FRIED FISH

Preparation time: Nil
Total cooking time: 8 minutes
Serves 4

plain flour, for dusting
olive oil
4 white fish steaks, such as
swordfish or blue-eyed cod

**1** Sift the flour together with a little salt and pepper onto a dinner plate. Coat both sides of the fish steaks with seasoned flour, shaking off the excess.
**2** Heat about 3 mm (1/8 inch) oil in a frying pan until very hot. Put the fish into the hot oil immediately and cook for 3 minutes on one side, then turn and cook the other side for 2 minutes, or until the coating is crisp and well browned. Reduce the heat to low and

cook for a further 2–3 minutes, until the flesh flakes easily with a fork.
**3** Remove from the pan and drain briefly on paper towels, then serve straight away, perhaps with lemon wedges, sautéed potatoes and a salad.

**COOK'S FILE**

**Note:** Cook the fish in batches, if necessary. Don't overcrowd the pan or the temperature will be reduced.

*Coat both sides of the fish with seasoned flour and shake off the excess.*

*Cook the fish for 3 minutes, then turn over. Cook in batches if necessary.*

*Remove from the pan and drain briefly on paper towels.*

## TROUT WITH LEEK AND CAPER SAUCE

Preparation time: 10 minutes
Total cooking time: 10 minutes
Serves 4

45 g (1½ oz) melted butter
4 thick ocean trout fillets
 (about 155 g/5 oz each)

*Leek and Caper Sauce*
50 g (1⅔ oz) butter

1 leek, chopped
1 cup (250 ml/8 fl oz) white
 wine (riesling or chardonnay)
2 tablespoons capers, drained
1 tablespoon chopped flat-leaf
 parsley

**1** Brush a shallow oven tray with melted butter and put the fish on the tray. Brush with melted butter and grill under moderate heat, without turning, until the fish is just cooked. Remove and cover loosely with foil to keep warm while making the sauce.

**2** To make Leek and Caper Sauce: Melt the butter in a pan and cook the leek gently until soft, but not brown. Add the wine and simmer for 3–4 minutes. Add the capers and parsley and salt and pepper to taste, then remove from the heat.

**3** Spoon the hot sauce over the fish and serve immediately.

### COOK'S FILE

**Variation:** Use salmon fillets or cutlets or any thick white fish instead of trout.

*Cut down the sides of the leek (not all the way to the base) to wash thoroughly.*

*Brush the trout with melted butter and grill until almost cooked.*

*Add the capers, parsley, salt and pepper, then remove from the heat.*

Once the mussels have cooled a little, remove them from their shells.

Mix the tomato paste with water and whisk into the simmering liquid.

Gradually add the milk, stirring constantly over low heat until thickened.

Spoon the White Sauce over the mussels and Tomato Sauce.

## MUSSELS IN TWO SAUCES

Preparation time: 25 minutes
Total cooking time: 45 minutes
Serves 4

3 tablespoons olive oil
1.25 kg (2½ lb) mussels in
   shells, scrubbed
3 tablespoons grated mozzarella
2 tablespoons grated Parmesan

*Tomato Sauce*
2 cloves garlic, crushed
½ cup (125 ml/4 fl oz) white
   wine
3 tablespoons tomato paste

*White Sauce*
25 g (¾ oz) butter
¼ cup (30 g/1 oz) plain flour
1 cup (250 ml/8 fl oz) milk

**1** Heat half the oil in a large pan. Add the mussels and cook over high heat, shaking the pan, for 5 minutes until opened. Discard any that do not open. Strain the liquid and reserve. Let the mussels cool, then remove from their shells. Preheat the oven to moderately hot 190°C (375°F/Gas 5).
**2 To make Tomato Sauce:** Heat the remaining oil in a pan. Add the garlic and fry until golden. Add the wine and reserved liquid and simmer gently for 5 minutes. Mix the tomato paste with 3 tablespoons water, then whisk into the simmering liquid. Simmer for a further 10 minutes and season to taste with salt and pepper.
**3 To make White Sauce:** Melt the butter in a pan. Add the flour and cook for 1 minute. Very gradually stir in the milk over low heat until the sauce thickens. Season.
**4** Combine the Tomato Sauce and mussels and pour into four 1-cup

(250 ml/8 fl oz) ramekins. Spoon over the White Sauce. Sprinkle with the combined cheeses and bake for 20 minutes. Serve with crusty bread.

# MEAT AND CHICKEN

## OLIVE AND LEMON LAMB CUTLETS

Preparation time: 15 minutes + marinating
Total cooking time: 10 minutes
Serves 4

12 lamb cutlets
2 tablespoons olive oil
juice and zest of 1 lemon
1 clove garlic, crushed
1 teaspoon finely chopped fresh rosemary leaves
1 teaspoon butter
16 black olives, cut into strips
2 tablespoons chopped parsley

**1** Trim the lamb cutlets of fat and place in a dish. Pour over 1 tablespoon of the oil, the lemon juice and zest, garlic and chopped rosemary. Leave to marinate for at least 30 minutes.
**2** Heat the remaining oil and the butter in a large frying pan. Drain the cutlets, reserving the marinade, and fry over medium heat until cooked through, turning once. Remove from the pan and set aside.
**3** Drain the excess fat from the pan and add the olives, parsley and remaining marinade. Bring to the boil and cook for 2 minutes. Season to taste with salt and pepper, pour over the cutlets and serve with mashed or roasted potatoes.

*Trim the fat away from the lamb cutlets, leaving just the meat and bone.*

*Pour over 1 tablespoon of oil, the lemon juice and zest, garlic and rosemary.*

*Fry the cutlets over medium heat until they are cooked through, turning once.*

*Add the olives, parsley and remaining marinade and cook for 2 minutes.*

## SPRING CHICKEN WITH HONEY GLAZE

Preparation time: 15 minutes
Total cooking time: 55 minutes
Serves 6–8

2 small (1.5 kg/3 lb) chickens
1 tablespoon light olive oil

*Honey Glaze*
3 tablespoons honey
juice and finely grated rind of
    1 lemon

1 tablespoon finely chopped
    rosemary
1 tablespoon dry white wine
1 tablespoon white wine vinegar
2 teaspoons Dijon mustard
1 1/2 tablespoons olive oil

**1** Preheat the oven to moderate 180°C (350°F/Gas 4). Halve the chickens by cutting down either side of the backbone. Discard the backbones. Cut the chickens into quarters; brush with oil and season lightly. Place on a rack in a roasting pan, skin-side-down, and roast for 20 minutes.

**2 To make Honey Glaze:** Combine all the ingredients in a small pan. Bring to the boil, reduce the heat and simmer for 5 minutes.

**3** After cooking one side, turn the chickens over and baste well with the warm glaze. Return to the oven and roast for 20 minutes. Baste once more and cook for a further 15 minutes. Serve hot or cold.

### COOK'S FILE

**Note:** To test if the chicken is cooked, pierce the meat at its thickest point. The juices should run clear.

*Halve each chicken by cutting down either side of the backbone.*

*Cut the chickens into quarters—you will find kitchen scissors easier than a knife.*

*Cook one side of the chicken, then turn over and baste with warm glaze.*

## PORK WITH MUSTARD AND CREAM SAUCE

Preparation time: 10 minutes
Total cooking time: 25 minutes
Serves 4

2 tablespoons olive oil
4 pork leg steaks
1 onion, sliced into rings

2 cloves garlic, crushed
1/2 cup (125 ml/4 fl oz) white wine
1 cup (250 ml/8 fl oz) cream
2 tablespoons wholegrain mustard
2 tablespoons chopped parsley

**1** Heat the oil in a large frying pan; cook the pork for 3–4 minutes each side. Transfer to a plate and set aside.

**2** Reduce the heat and add the onion. Cook until soft, then add the garlic and cook for 1 minute further. Add the wine and simmer until the liquid is reduced by half.

**3** Stir in the cream and mustard and simmer gently for 5 minutes. Add the pork and simmer for a further 5 minutes. Stir in the parsley and season to taste. Serve immediately, the sauce spooned over the pork.

*Fry the pork in oil for 3–4 minutes on each side, until browned.*

*Cook the onion and garlic until soft and golden, then add the wine and simmer.*

*Add the pork and then simmer gently for 5 minutes. Stir in the fresh parsley.*

## LEG OF LAMB WITH PANCETTA STUFFING

Preparation time: 30 minutes
Total cooking time: 1 hour 45 minutes
Serves 6

60 g (2 oz) pancetta, chopped
60 g (2 oz) mild Provolone
   cheese, chopped
2 tablespoons grated Parmesan
1/3 cup (25 g/3/4 oz) fresh
   breadcrumbs
3 tablespoons chopped fresh
   flat-leaf parsley
2 teaspoons chopped fresh
   rosemary
2 spring onions, chopped
1 egg plus 1 yolk, lightly beaten
1.5 kg (3 lb) boned leg of lamb
   (ask your butcher to do this)
3 tablespoons olive oil
1 onion, chopped
1 carrot, chopped
1 celery stick, chopped
1 cup (250 ml/8 fl oz) dry white
   wine
1 tablespoon plain flour

**1** Preheat the oven to moderately hot 200°C (400°F/Gas 6). Combine the pancetta, cheeses, breadcrumbs, herbs, spring onions and enough beaten egg to form a stuffing that just comes together. Season with pepper.

**2** Fill the lamb leg with stuffing, fold over the ends and secure with wooden skewers or string.

**3** Heat the oil in a large deep pan and brown the lamb all over. Transfer to a baking dish and sprinkle with salt and pepper. Reheat the pan and add the onion, carrot and celery; toss over the heat for 2 minutes. Add the wine, let the bubbles subside, then pour over the lamb. Bake for 1 1/2 hours, or until tender, turning once or twice.

**4** Remove the meat from the dish and leave, loosely covered, for 10 minutes before slicing. Strain the pan juices into a jug and skim off the fat; add water to make up 1 1/2 cups (375 ml/12 fl oz). Heat the flour in a small pan until beginning to brown, remove from the heat and slowly whisk in the pan juices until smooth. Return to the heat and whisk until the sauce boils and thickens. Return the vegetables to the sauce and drizzle over the meat.

*Add enough beaten egg to the stuffing mixture to make it just stick together.*

*Carefully stuff the leg of lamb, pushing the pancetta filling into the cavity.*

*Skewer together the open ends of the leg of lamb, or tie with string.*

*Use a large deep pan to brown the lamb as the fat will tend to spit.*

## VEAL SCALOPPINI WITH LEMON SAUCE

Preparation time: 5 minutes
Total cooking time: 5 minutes
Serves 4

3 tablespoons olive oil
60 g (2 oz) butter
8 thin veal steaks
plain flour, for coating
2 tablespoons lemon juice

2 tablespoons finely chopped
 parsley
lemon slices, to garnish

**1** Heat the oil and half the butter in a large frying pan until quite hot. Coat the veal steaks in the flour and add to the pan, cooking in batches if necessary. Cook until lightly browned on one side, then turn over and brown the other side. The veal steaks should take only 1 minute on each side—cooking longer will toughen the meat.

Transfer to a warm plate and season with salt and pepper.
**2** Lower the heat and add the lemon juice, parsley and remaining butter to the pan, stirring to combine. Add the veal steaks, turning them in the sauce.
**3** Serve the veal steaks with the sauce. Garnish with lemon slices.

### COOK'S FILE

**Note:** For thin veal steaks, cover them with plastic wrap and beat with a rolling pin or meat mallet.

Coat the veal steaks in flour, shaking off any excess.

Lightly brown the veal steaks on either side, cooking in batches if necessary.

Return all the veal steaks to the pan, turning to coat them in sauce.

# BEEF WITH PROSCIUTTO AND MUSHROOMS

Preparation time: 15 minutes
Total cooking time: 25 minutes
Serves 4

2 tablespoons olive oil
200 g (6¹/2 oz) button
mushrooms, stalks trimmed
60 g (2 oz) sliced prosciutto, cut
into wide strips
4 thick slices beef scotch fillet
or eye fillet steaks

2 cloves garlic, crushed
2 tablespoons chopped fresh
flat-leaf parsley
¹/4 cup (60 ml/2 fl oz) dry white
wine
¹/2 cup (125 ml/4 fl oz) cream

**1** Preheat the oven to moderately hot 200°C (400°F/Gas 6). Heat the oil in a deep ovenproof frying pan (large enough to hold the beef steaks in one layer, without overlapping). Add the mushrooms and prosciutto and toss until the mushrooms start to brown.
**2** Layer the steaks over the

mushrooms, sprinkle with garlic and parsley, then pour over the wine. Bring to the boil, reduce the heat, then cover the pan (with a lid or tightly with foil) and bake for 10–15 minutes, or until the steaks are cooked to taste.
**3** Set the steaks aside to keep warm. Heat the pan on the hotplate, add the cream and boil for 3–5 minutes, or until thickened slightly; pour over the steaks and serve immediately.

### COOK'S FILE

**Note:** Flat-leaf parsley is also known as Italian or continental parsley.

*Add the mushrooms and prosciutto to the oil and toss until starting to brown.*

*Sprinkle the steaks with garlic and parsley and then pour in the wine.*

*Add the cream to the pan and boil for 3–5 minutes, or until slightly thickened.*

*Trim away any fat from the veal cutlets, then toss them in flour.*

*Cook the veal cutlets in a single layer until browned on both sides.*

*Once most of the wine has evaporated, pour in the beef stock and add pepper.*

*If the pan juices need thickening, simmer them for a while, uncovered.*

## VEAL CUTLETS WITH SAGE

Preparation time: 25 minutes
Total cooking time: 1 hour 20 minutes
Serves 4–6

8 veal cutlets
2–3 tablespoons plain flour
30 g (1 oz) butter
2 tablespoons olive oil
75 g (2½ oz) sliced ham, cut
   into strips
½ cup (125 ml/4 fl oz) dry
   white wine
8 fresh sage leaves, shredded
2 teaspoons chopped fresh
   rosemary
1 cup (250 ml/8 fl oz) beef
   stock
freshly ground black pepper

**1** Trim any fat from the veal cutlets and then toss in flour. Shake off the excess flour.
**2** Heat the butter and 1 tablespoon of the oil in a large baking dish. When foaming, add the veal cutlets in a single layer and cook until browned on both sides. Drain on paper towels. Wipe the pan clean, then add the remaining oil and the ham; toss over the heat for a few minutes.
**3** Return the cutlets to the pan, then pour in the wine with the herbs. Simmer, uncovered, until most of the liquid has evaporated. Add the stock and black pepper. Bring back to the boil, reduce the heat and simmer, covered (with foil if necessary), for about 1 hour, or until the cutlets are tender, turning once during cooking.
**4** Transfer the cutlets to a serving dish and keep warm. If the pan juices

are very thin, simmer uncovered until thickened. Season with salt to taste, if necessary, then pour over the cutlets. Garnish with fresh sage.

## BEEF OLIVES WITH ARTICHOKE STUFFING

Preparation time: 20 minutes
Total cooking time: 50 minutes
Serves 4

8 slices beef topside (about
    80 g/2²/₃ oz each slice)
100 g (3¹/₃ oz) prosciutto, finely
    chopped
50 g (1²/₃ oz) butter, melted
4 artichoke hearts
2 tablespoons chopped fresh
    thyme
plain flour, for coating
¹/₃ cup (80 ml/2³/₄ fl oz) dry
    white wine
¹/₂ cup (125 ml/4 fl oz) beef
    stock

**1** Flatten each beef slice with a meat mallet (or rolling pin) until wafer thin. Mix together the prosciutto and 1 tablespoon of the butter and spread over the beef slices. Roughly chop each artichoke into quarters and arrange the pieces evenly over the prosciutto. Sprinkle with thyme and salt and pepper to taste.

**2** Roll up the beef slices around the stuffing. Tie each Beef Olive with string to hold it together.

**3** Heat the remaining butter in a frying pan. Roll the Beef Olives in a little flour, shake off the excess and fry until browned. Add the wine and the beef stock, then cover and cook for 45 minutes, or until tender. Turn the meat several times during cooking.

**4** Remove the Beef Olives with a slotted spoon, cover and keep warm. Return the pan to the heat and reduce the sauce until slightly thickened, if necessary. Season to taste with salt and black pepper. Remove the string from the Beef Olives and pour the sauce over before serving.

### COOK'S FILE

**Note:** To make beef stock at home, bake 2 kg (4 lb) beef bones at 210°C (415°F/Gas 6–7) for 30 minutes, then simmer in a large pan with chopped carrots, onions, celery, bouquet garni and 3 litres water for 4 hours. Ready-made stock in a tetra pack is very convenient but can be salty—try using half stock, half water.

*Cover the beef with a sheet of plastic wrap and flatten with a meat mallet.*

*Roll the beef around the filling and then secure with string.*

*Add the wine, a little more salt and black pepper and the beef stock.*

*Remove the Beef Olives from the pan, then reduce the sauce to thicken.*

## CHICKEN MARSALA

Preparation time: 10 minutes
Total cooking time: 25 minutes
Serves 4

4 chicken breast fillets
2 tablespoons oil
60 g (2 oz) butter
1 clove garlic, crushed
2 cups (500 ml/16 fl oz) chicken
   stock
1/3 cup (80 ml/2³/4 fl oz) Marsala
2 teaspoons plain flour
3 tablespoons cream
2 teaspoons Worcestershire
   sauce

**1** Trim the chicken of excess fat and sinew. Heat the oil in a heavy-based frying pan and add the chicken. Cook over medium heat for 4 minutes on each side, or until cooked through and lightly golden. Remove the chicken, cover loosely with foil and keep warm. Drain off any fat from the pan.
**2** Add the butter and garlic to the pan and stir over medium heat for 2 minutes. Add the combined stock and Marsala and bring to the boil. Reduce the heat and simmer for 10 minutes, or until the liquid has reduced by half.
**3** Blend together the flour, cream and Worcestershire sauce; add a little of the hot liquid and blend to a paste.

Add this to the pan and then stir over medium heat until the sauce boils and thickens. Season to taste with salt and black pepper and then pour over the chicken fillets. Delicious with pasta.

**COOK'S FILE**

**Variation:** Marsala is a sweet wine and so makes a sweet-tasting sauce. Port or any dry red wine can be used instead. Boiling wine evaporates the alcohol, leaving the flavour but not the intoxicating qualities. Chicken thighs or drumsticks can be used instead of breast fillets.
**Hint:** Blending the flour to a paste first prevents lumps forming when it is added to the sauce.

*Cook the chicken in a frying pan until lightly golden on each side.*

*Mix together the stock and Marsala, then add to the pan and bring to the boil.*

*Add the flour, cream and Worcestershire sauce and stir over heat until thickened.*

## CHICKEN CACCIATORE

Preparation time: 20 minutes
Total cooking time: 1 hour
Serves 6

3 tablespoons olive oil
12 small chicken drumsticks
1 large onion, finely chopped
3 cloves garlic, crushed
440 g (14 oz) can crushed
　　tomatoes
1/2 cup (90 g/3 oz) black olives

1 cup (250 ml/8 fl oz) tomato
　　purée
1/2 cup (125 ml/4 fl oz) white
　　wine
1/2 cup (125 ml/4 fl oz) chicken
　　stock
125 g (4 oz) button mushrooms,
　　quartered
1 tablespoon chopped fresh
　　oregano
2 teaspoons chopped fresh
　　thyme
2 teaspoons soft brown
　　sugar

**1** Heat half the oil in a large heavy-based pan and brown the drumsticks in small batches over high heat.
**2** Heat the remaining oil in a frying pan and cook the onion and garlic for 10 minutes, or until golden. Remove from the pan and add to the chicken.
**3** Add the remaining ingredients to the frying pan. Bring to the boil, reduce the heat and then simmer for 10 minutes. Season to taste with salt and pepper. Pour over the chicken, stir to combine, cover and simmer for 35 minutes, or until very tender.

*Cut the mushrooms into quarters and finely chop the onion.*

*Cook the drumsticks in batches so they brown—if overcrowded they will stew.*

*Simmer the tomato mixture, then pour over the chicken and mix together.*

## LAMB SHANKS WITH LENTILS

Preparation time: 20 minutes
Total cooking time: 2 hours
Serves 2

1 cup (250 g/8 oz) red lentils,
　　rinsed and drained
1/2 teaspoon salt
2 celery sticks, diced
1 green capsicum, diced
2 cloves garlic, finely chopped
2 onions, finely chopped
4 small lamb shanks

800 g (1 lb 10 oz) can crushed
　　tomatoes
3 bay leaves
3 teaspoons chopped fresh
　　marjoram
3 teaspoons chopped thyme

**1** Preheat the oven to moderate 180°C (350°F/Gas 4). Spread the lentils in the base of a large ovenproof casserole dish and sprinkle with salt.
**2** Add the celery, capsicum, garlic and onion. Layer the lamb shanks over the top, then pour over the tomatoes. Add the bay leaves, fresh marjoram and thyme. Cover the dish (with foil if you don't have a lid) and bake for 2 hours.
**3** Skim off any fat which may have formed on the surface. Remove the bay leaves and stir together the lentils, meat and vegetables before serving.

**C O O K ' S   F I L E**

**Note:** Red lentils are smaller and softer than green or brown lentils and so do not need to be soaked before cooking.
**Variation:** Lamb shanks are a very economical cut of meat—use chump chops if shanks are not available.

*Spread the lentils in a large dish and sprinkle with salt.*

*Place the vegetables over the lentils, layer the lamb on top and add the tomatoes.*

*Remove the bay leaves and give the dish a quick stir before serving.*

*Chicken Cacciatore (top)*
*and Lamb Shanks with Lentils*

## OSSO BUCCO

Preparation time: 30 minutes
Total cooking time: 2 hours 50 minutes
Serves 4–6

2 tablespoons plain flour
freshly ground black pepper
4 veal shanks (osso bucco), cut
    into short lengths
2 tablespoons oil
2 cloves garlic, crushed
1 large onion, chopped
1 large carrot, chopped
2/3 cup (170 ml/5¹/2 fl oz) dry
    white wine
2/3 cup (170 ml/5¹/2 fl oz) beef
    stock
425 g (13¹/2 oz) can tomatoes
3 tablespoons tomato paste
¹/2 teaspoon caster sugar

*Gremolata*
¹/3 cup (7 g/¹/4 oz) fresh parsley
1 clove garlic, crushed
2 teaspoons grated lemon rind

**1** Preheat the oven to moderate 180°C (350°F/Gas 4). Lightly grease a 12-cup (3-litre) baking dish. Combine the flour and pepper on a sheet of greaseproof paper and lightly coat the osso bucco. Shake off the excess.
**2** Heat the oil in a heavy-based pan. Brown the meat on both sides over medium-high heat; drain on paper towels. Transfer to the baking dish.
**3** Add the garlic and onion to the pan and cook, stirring, until just soft. Add the carrot, wine, stock, crushed tomatoes, tomato paste and sugar. Bring to the boil, reduce the heat and simmer for 5 minutes. Spoon over the meat, cover with foil and bake for 2 hours. Uncover and bake for a further 30 minutes, or until tender.
**4 To make Gremolata:** Finely chop the parsley, then mix with the garlic and rind. Just before serving, sprinkle Gremolata over Osso Bucco.

### COOK'S FILE

**Storage time:** Cook Osso Bucco up to 1 day ahead and keep, covered, in the refrigerator, or freeze for 1 month. Make Gremolata just before serving.
**Note:** This is a very traditional dish—the marrow in the bone adds flavour to the recipe.

*Put the flour and pepper on greaseproof paper and lightly coat the osso bucco.*

*Brown the meat in batches—if the pan is overcrowded it will stew rather than fry.*

*Spoon the tomato mixture over the meat, cover with foil and bake until tender.*

*Finely chop the parsley and mix together with the garlic and lemon rind.*

## PESTO LAMB CUTLETS

Preparation time: 40 minutes + chilling
Total cooking time: 20 minutes
Serves 4

12 lamb cutlets
1 egg
3 tablespoons pesto
1 teaspoon wholegrain
   mustard
2 tablespoons cornflour

1 cup (80 g/2²/3 oz) fresh
   breadcrumbs
1/3 cup (35 g/1¹/4 oz) grated
   Parmesan
1/3 cup (50 g/1²/3 oz) pine nuts,
   finely chopped

**1** Trim any fat from the cutlets and scrape the flesh from the bone to give them a nice shape. Whisk together the egg, pesto, mustard and cornflour.
**2** Mix the breadcrumbs, Parmesan and pine nuts in a bowl. Dip each cutlet into the pesto then breadcrumb mixtures. Chill for 30 minutes.
**3** Shallow-fry the cutlets in oil, in batches, for 5 minutes each side.

### COOK'S FILE

**Note:** To make pesto, process 2 bunches basil leaves, 4 tablespoons toasted pine nuts, 2 crushed cloves garlic and 4 tablespoons grated Parmesan until finely chopped. Still processing, slowly add 4 tablespoons olive oil in a stream, until well mixed.

*Whisk together the egg, pesto, mustard and cornflour.*

*Dip the cutlets in the pesto mixture, then the breadcrumb mixture.*

*Turn the cutlets with a spatula, taking care not to dislodge the crumb coating.*

## ROAST GARLIC CHICKEN WITH VEGETABLES

Preparation time: 20 minutes
Total cooking time: 1 hour 20 minutes
Serves 4

315 g (10 oz) orange sweet potatoes, peeled and cut into wedges
315 g (10 oz) pontiac potatoes, peeled and cut into wedges
315 g (10 oz) pumpkin, peeled and cut into wedges

1 chicken, cut into 8 pieces, or 1.5 kg (3 lb) chicken pieces
3 tablespoons olive oil
1 tablespoon fresh thyme leaves
20 large garlic cloves, unpeeled (see note)
1/2 teaspoon sea salt

**1** Preheat the oven to hot 220°C (425°F/Gas 7). Bring a large pan of salted water to the boil and cook the sweet potatoes, pontiac potatoes and pumpkin for 5 minutes. Drain well.
**2** Put the chicken and vegetables in a baking dish, drizzle with olive oil and scatter with thyme leaves and garlic cloves. Sprinkle with the sea salt.
**3** Roast for 1 hour 15 minutes, turning every 20 minutes or so, until the chicken, potatoes and pumpkin become well browned and crisp at the edges. Serve immediately.

### COOK'S FILE

**Note:** This may seem an awful lot of garlic, but it loses its pungency when cooked, becoming sweet and mild. To eat the garlic, squeeze the creamy roasted flesh from the skins and over the chicken and vegetables.

*Boil the sweet and pontiac potatoes and pumpkin for 5 minutes, then drain.*

*Drizzle the chicken and vegetables with oil then sprinkle with garlic and thyme.*

*Turn the chicken and vegetables every 20 minutes, until browned and crisp.*

Use a meat mallet to flatten the veal steaks. Nick the edges to prevent curling.

Press the crumb mixture firmly onto the steaks with your fingers to make it stick.

Cook the steaks in batches until golden brown, then drain on paper towels.

Top with the Parmesan and mozzarella and bake until golden brown.

## VEAL PARMIGIANA

Preparation time: 30 minutes + chilling
Total cooking time: 30 minutes
Serves 4

4 thin veal steaks
1 cup (100 g/3¹/3 oz) dry
    breadcrumbs
¹/2 teaspoon dried basil
¹/4 cup (25 g/³/4 oz) finely grated
    fresh Parmesan
plain flour, for coating
1 egg, lightly beaten
1 tablespoon milk
oilve oil, for frying
1 cup (250 g/8 oz) good-quality
    ready-made tomato pasta
    sauce
¹/2 cup (50 g/1²/3 oz) finely
    grated fresh Parmesan, extra
100 g (3¹/3 oz) mozzarella,
    thinly sliced

**1** Trim the meat of any excess fat and sinew. Place between sheets of plastic wrap and flatten with a meat mallet to 5 mm (¹/4 inch) thick. Nick the edges to prevent curling. Combine the breadcrumbs, basil and Parmesan on a sheet of greaseproof paper.
**2** Coat the veal steaks in flour, shaking off the excess. Working with one at a time, dip the steaks into the combined egg and milk, then coat with the breadcrumb mixture. Lightly shake off the excess. Refrigerate for 30 minutes to firm the coating.
**3** Preheat the oven to moderate 180°C (350°F/Gas 4). Heat the oil in a frying pan and brown the veal steaks over medium heat for 2 minutes each side, in batches if necessary. Drain on paper towels.
**4** Spread half the pasta sauce into a shallow ovenproof dish. Arrange the veal steaks on top in a single layer and spoon over the remaining sauce.

Top with the Parmesan cheese and mozzarella and bake for 20 minutes, or until the cheeses are melted and golden brown. Serve immediately.

# RISOTTO, POLENTA AND BREAD

## PRAWN SAFFRON RISOTTO

Preparation time: 20 minutes
Total cooking time: 40 minutes
Serves 4

1/4 teaspoon saffron threads
500 g (1 lb) raw prawns
1/3 cup (80 ml/2³/4 fl oz) olive oil
2 cloves garlic, crushed
3 tablespoons chopped parsley
3 tablespoons dry sherry
3 tablespoons white wine
6 cups (1.5 litres) fish stock
1 onion, diced
2 cups (440g/14 oz) arborio
   rice

**1** Soak the saffron threads in 3 tablespoons water. Peel the prawns and devein, leaving the tails intact. Heat 2 tablespoons of the olive oil in a pan. Add the garlic, parsley and prawns and season with salt and pepper, to taste. Cook for 2 minutes, then add the sherry, wine and saffron threads with their liquid. Remove the prawns with a slotted spoon. Simmer until the liquid has reduced by half. Add the fish stock and 1 cup (250 ml/ 8 fl oz) water and leave to simmer.

**2** In a separate large, heavy-based pan heat the remaining oil. Add the onion and rice and cook for 3 minutes. Keeping the pan of stock constantly at simmering point, add 1/2 cup (125 ml/ 4 oz) hot stock to the rice mixture. Stir constantly over low heat, with a wooden spoon, until all the liquid has been absorbed. Add another half cupful of stock and repeat the process until all the stock has been added and the rice is tender and creamy—this will take 25–30 minutes.

**3** Stir in the prawns, warm through and serve, perhaps with freshly grated Parmesan cheese.

### COOK'S FILE

**Note:** Saffron is the most expensive spice in the world but only a very tiny amount is necessary.

*Cook the prawns for 2 minutes, then remove with a slotted spoon.*

*Keep the stock simmering in a separate pan and add a little at a time.*

## CARAWAY POLENTA WITH BRAISED LEEKS

Preparation time: 10 minutes
Total cooking time: 30 minutes
Serves 4

6 cups (1.5 litres) chicken stock
1 1/2 cups (225 g/7 1/2 oz) polenta
2 teaspoons caraway seeds
45 g (1 1/2 oz) butter
2 large leeks, cut into thin strips

250 g (8 oz) Italian Fontina cheese, cut into cubes

**1** Place the stock in a large heavy-based pan and bring to the boil. Pour in the polenta in a fine stream, stirring continuously. Add the caraway seeds and then reduce the heat and simmer for about 20–25 minutes, or until the polenta is very soft.
**2** Melt the butter in a frying pan over moderate heat and add the leeks. Cover and cook gently, stirring occasionally, until wilted. Add the Fontina cubes, stir a couple of times and remove from the heat.
**3** Pour the polenta onto individual plates in nest shapes and spoon the leeks and cheese into the centre.

### COOK'S FILE

**Hint:** Ready-made stock can be quite salty, so use half stock, half water.
**Note:** Polenta is also known as cornmeal and is available from most supermarkets and delicatessens.

*Use a sharp knife to cut the leeks into very thin, long strips.*

*Bring the stock to the boil, then pour in the polenta, stirring continuously.*

*Cook the leeks in the butter until wilted, then stir in the cheese.*

*When the pancetta starts to curl at the edges, add the peas and half the wine.*

*Put the stock and water in a separate pan and keep at simmering point.*

*Fry the onion in the butter and then add the rice and stir until well combined.*

*Once the rice is cooked, stir in the pea mixture and Parmesan cheese.*

## PEA AND PANCETTA RISOTTO

Preparation time: 25 minutes
Total cooking time: 45 minutes
Serves 4

1 tablespoon olive oil
1 celery stick, chopped
2 tablespoons chopped fresh
 flat-leaf parsley
freshly ground black pepper
75 g (2¹/₂ oz) sliced pancetta,
 coarsely chopped
250 g (8 oz) peas (fresh or
 frozen)
¹/₂ cup (125 ml/4 fl oz) dry
 white wine
3 cups (750 ml/24 fl oz) chicken
 stock
60 g (2 oz) butter
1 onion, chopped
2 cups (440 g/14 oz) arborio
 rice
¹/₃ cup (35 g/1¹/₄ oz) freshly
 grated Parmesan

**1** Heat the oil in a frying pan, add the celery, parsley and black pepper and cook over medium heat for a few minutes to soften the celery. Add the pancetta and stir until it just begins to curl. Add the peas and half the wine, bring to the boil, then reduce the heat and simmer uncovered until almost all the liquid has evaporated. Set aside.
**2** Put the stock and 3 cups (750 ml/ 24 fl oz) water in a separate pan and keep at simmering point.
**3** Heat the butter in a large heavy-based saucepan. Add the onion and stir until softened. Add the rice and stir well. Pour in the remaining wine; allow it to bubble and evaporate. Add ¹/₂ cup (125 ml/4 oz) hot stock to the rice mixture. Stir constantly over low heat, with a wooden spoon, until all the stock has been absorbed. Repeat the process until all the stock has been added and the rice is creamy and tender (about 25–30 minutes).
**4** Add the pea mixture and Parmesan and serve immediately. Serve with Parmesan shavings and black pepper.

### COOK'S FILE

**Note:** If fresh peas are in season, 500 g (1 lb) peas in the pod will yield about 250 g (8 oz) shelled peas.

## CARROT AND PUMPKIN RISOTTO

Preparation time: 15 minutes
Total cooking time: 35 minutes
Serves 4

90 g (3 oz) butter
1 onion, finely chopped
250 g (8 oz) pumpkin, peeled
   and cut into small cubes
2 carrots, cut into small cubes
7–8 cups (1.75–2 litres)
   vegetable stock

2 cups (440 g/14 oz) arborio
   rice
90 g (3 oz) freshly grated
   Romano cheese
1/4 teaspoon nutmeg
freshly ground black pepper

**1** Heat 60 g (2 oz) of the butter in a large, heavy-based pan. Add the onion and fry for 1–2 minutes, or until soft. Add the pumpkin and carrot and cook for 6–8 minutes, or until tender. Mash slightly with a potato masher. In a separate saucepan keep the stock at simmering point.

**2** Add the rice to the vegetables and cook for 1 minute, stirring constantly. Ladle in enough hot stock to cover the rice; stir well. Reduce the heat and add more stock as it is absorbed, stirring frequently. Continue until the rice is tender and creamy (about 25 minutes).

**3** Remove from the heat, add the remaining butter, cheese, nutmeg and pepper and fork through. Cover and leave for 5 minutes before serving.

### COOK'S FILE

**Note:** Romano is a hard, grating cheese similar to Parmesan.

*Heat the butter in a large pan and fry the onion until soft.*

*Cook the pumpkin and carrot until tender, then mash a little.*

*The secret to good risotto is to add the stock a little at a time and stir often.*

*Add the polenta to the stock and water and stir constantly until very thick.*

*Use the back of a spoon to spread the polenta in the tin.*

*Build up the layers of sliced polenta, butter and cheese.*

*Add the final layer of sliced polenta and then sprinkle with Parmesan cheese.*

## BAKED POLENTA WITH THREE CHEESES

Preparation time: 20 minutes
  + 2 hours chilling
Total cooking time: 45 minutes
Serves 4

*Polenta*
2¹/₂ cups (600 ml/20 fl oz)
  chicken stock
2 cups (300 g/9²/₃ oz) polenta
¹/₂ cup (50 g/2²/₃ oz) freshly
  grated Parmesan

*Cheese Filling*
100 g (3¹/₃ oz) havarti cheese,
  sliced
100 g (3¹/₃ oz) mascarpone
100 g (3¹/₃ oz) blue cheese,
  crumbled
100 g (3¹/₃ oz) butter, sliced
  thinly
¹/₂ cup (50 g/1²/₃ oz) freshly
  grated Parmesan

**1** **To make Polenta:** Brush a 7-cup (1.75 litre) loaf tin with oil. Put the stock and 2 cups (500 ml/16 fl oz) water in a large pan and bring to the boil. Add the polenta and stir for 10 minutes until very thick.
**2** Remove from the heat and stir in the Parmesan. Spread into the tin and smooth the surface. Refrigerate for 2 hours, then cut into about 30 thin slices. Preheat the oven to moderate 180°C (350°F/Gas 4).
**3** Brush a large ovenproof dish with oil. Place a layer of polenta slices on the base. Top with a layer of half the combined havarti, mascarpone and blue cheeses and half the butter. Add another layer of polenta and top with the remainder of the three cheeses and butter. Add a final layer of polenta and sprinkle the Parmesan on top. Bake for 30 minutes, or until a golden crust forms. Serve immediately.

### COOK'S FILE

**Note:** Polenta is also known as cornmeal and is available from most supermarkets and delicatessens.
**Note:** Havarti is actually a Danish cheese with a full flavour.

## SUN-DRIED TOMATO ROLLS

Preparation time: 20 minutes + resting
Total cooking time: 40 minutes
Makes 16 rolls

3 tablespoons olive oil
2 red onions, sliced
1 tablespoon tomato paste
2/3 cup (110 g/3²/3 oz) sun-dried
    tomatoes, chopped
1 tablespoon chopped fresh
    oregano
2 teaspoons chopped fresh
    rosemary
1/4 teaspoon dried chilli flakes
14 g (1/2 oz) packet dried yeast
6 cups (750 g/1¹/2 lb) plain flour
3 teaspoons salt
2 tablespoons polenta
1 egg white, lightly beaten

**1** Heat the oil in a pan and cook the onions until very soft. Stir in the tomato paste, tomatoes, herbs and chilli. Cool to room temperature.

**2** Put the yeast, 1 cup (250 ml/8 fl oz) warm water and 1 cup (125 g/4 oz) of the flour in a bowl, then whisk until smooth and leave in a warm place for 20 minutes, or until frothy.

**3** Sift the remaining flour and the salt into a large bowl. Make a well in the centre and pour in the yeast mixture, 1 cup (250 ml/8 fl oz) warm water and the tomato mixture. Gradually mix to form a soft sticky dough. Turn out onto a floured surface and knead for 5 minutes. Place in a greased bowl, cover loosely with greased plastic wrap and leave in a warm place for 1 hour, or until doubled. Grease two 20 cm (8 inch) round shallow cake tins and sprinkle with a little polenta.

**4** Punch down the dough, then knead on a floured surface for 3 minutes. Divide into 16 portions. Roll into balls and arrange in the cake tins. Make 2–3 cuts on the top of each roll. Leave in a warm place for 20 minutes or until risen; brush with egg white and sprinkle with polenta. Preheat the oven to 200°C (400°F/Gas 6).

**5** Bake for 30 minutes (cover with foil if overbrowning). For crusty bread rolls, spray with a little water about three times during baking. Turn out onto a wire rack and serve.

*Whisk the yeast, water and flour together and leave in a warm place until frothy.*

*Add the yeast mixture, warm water and tomato mixture to the flour.*

*Leave the dough in a warm place for 1 hour, or until doubled in size.*

*Divide the dough into 16 portions, then roll into balls and put in the tins.*

## GRILLED POLENTA WITH WILD MUSHROOMS

Preparation time: 30 minutes + chilling
Total cooking time: 1 hour 20 minutes
Serves 6–8

*Polenta*
2¹/2 cups (600 ml/20 fl oz) chicken stock
2 cups (300 g/9²/3 oz) polenta
1 cup (100 g/3¹/3 oz) freshly grated Parmesan

*Mushroom Sauce*
1 kg (2 lb) mixed mushrooms (roman, oyster and flat)
¹/2 cup (125 ml/4 fl oz) olive oil
¹/2 cup (15 g/¹/2 oz) chopped parsley
4 cloves garlic, finely chopped
1 onion, chopped

**1 To make Polenta:** Put the stock and 2 cups (500 ml/16 fl oz) water in a large pan and bring to the boil. Add the polenta and stir constantly for 10 minutes until very thick. Remove from the heat and stir in the Parmesan. Brush a 20 cm (8 inch) round spring-form tin with oil. Spread the polenta into the tin and smooth the surface. Refrigerate for 2 hours, turn out and cut into 6–8 wedges.
**2 To make Mushroom Sauce:**

Wipe the mushrooms with a damp cloth and roughly chop the larger ones. Put the mushrooms, oil, parsley, garlic and onion in a pan. Stir, cover and leave to simmer for 50 minutes, or until cooked through. Uncover and cook for 10 minutes, or until there is very little liquid left. Set aside.
**3** Brush one side of the polenta with olive oil and cook under a preheated grill for 5 minutes, or until the edges are browned. Turn over and brown. Reheat the Mushroom Sauce and serve spooned over slices of polenta.

### COOK'S FILE

**Note:** Use just button mushrooms if the other varieties aren't available.

*Stir the polenta until very thick, remove from the heat and add the Parmesan.*

*Refrigerate for 2 hours, then turn out and cut into wedges.*

*Uncover the mushrooms and simmer for 10 minutes, until little liquid is left.*

# DESSERTS

## CHILLED ORANGE CREAMS

Preparation time: 30 minutes + chilling
Total cooking time: 5 minutes
Serves 6

½ cup (125 ml/4 fl oz) juice of
    blood oranges
3 teaspoons gelatine
4 egg yolks
½ cup (125 g/4 oz) caster sugar
1¼ cups (315 ml/10 fl oz) milk
1 teaspoon finely grated
    blood orange rind
1 cup (250 ml/8 fl oz) cream

**1** Put a large bowl in the freezer and chill. Put a few drops of almond or light olive oil on your fingertips and lightly grease the insides of six ½-cup (125 ml/4 fl oz) moulds. Put the orange juice in a small bowl and sprinkle with gelatine; set aside.

**2** Whisk the yolks and sugar in a small bowl until thick. Heat the milk and rind in a pan and gradually pour onto the egg mixture while whisking. Return to the pan and stir until the custard coats the back of the spoon— do not allow it to boil. Add the gelatine mixture and stir to dissolve.

**3** Pour the mixture immediately through a strainer into the chilled bowl. Cool, stirring occasionally, until beginning to thicken. Whip the cream into soft peaks and fold into the custard. Spoon into the moulds and chill to set. Serve with cream, if liked.

### COOK'S FILE

**Variation:** Blood oranges have a short season but they give the best colour. You could use navel or Valencia oranges, or mandarins.

*Put the blood orange juice in a small bowl and sprinkle with gelatine.*

*Stir the custard until it will coat the back of a spoon.*

*Pour the custard mixture through a strainer into the chilled bowl.*

*Whip the cream into soft peaks and then fold into the custard with a metal spoon.*

## PANNA COTTA WITH RUBY SAUCE

Preparation time: 20 minutes + chilling
Total cooking time: 20 minutes
Serves 6

1¹/₂ cups (375 ml/12 fl oz) milk
3 teaspoons gelatine
1¹/₂ cups (375 ml/12 fl oz)
    cream
¹/₃ cup (90 g/3 oz) caster sugar
2 tablespoons Amaretto liqueur

*Ruby Sauce*
1 cup (250 g/8 oz) caster sugar
1 cinnamon stick
1 cup fresh or frozen
    raspberries
¹/₂ cup (125 ml/4 fl oz) good-
    quality red wine

**1** Use your fingertips to lightly smear the inside of 6 individual 150 ml (5 fl oz) moulds with almond or light olive oil. Place 3 tablespoons of the milk in a small bowl and sprinkle with gelatine; leave to dissolve for a few minutes.

**2** Put the remaining milk in a pan with the cream and sugar and heat gently while stirring, until almost boiling. Remove the pan from the heat; whisk the gelatine into the cream mixture and whisk until dissolved. Leave to cool for 5 minutes and then stir in the Amaretto.

**3** Pour the mixture into the moulds and chill until set (about 4 hours). Unmould and serve with Ruby Sauce.

**4 To make Ruby Sauce:** Place the sugar and 1 cup (250 ml/8 fl oz) water in a pan and stir over medium heat until the sugar has completely dissolved (do not allow to boil). Add the cinnamon stick and simmer for 5 minutes. Add the raspberries and wine and boil rapidly for 5 minutes. Remove the cinnamon stick and push the sauce through a sieve; discard the seeds. Cool and then chill the sauce in the refrigerator before serving.

### COOK'S FILE

**Note:** If you prefer, replace the Amaretto with ¹/₂ teaspoon almond extract. The Panna Cotta will be a little firmer. This is delicious, and traditionally Italian, with fresh figs.

Put some of the milk into a small bowl and sprinkle with gelatine.

Whisk the dissolved gelatine into the cream mixture until dissolved.

Pour the mixture into the moulds and then refrigerate until set.

Remove the cinnamon stick and strain the sauce through a sieve.

## RICOTTA POTS WITH RASPBERRIES

Preparation time: 20 minutes
Total cooking time: 25 minutes
Serves 4

4 eggs, separated
1/2 cup (125 g/4 oz) caster sugar
350 g (11 1/4 oz) fresh ricotta
1/4 cup (35 g/1 1/4 oz) finely chopped pistachio nuts
1 teaspoon grated lemon rind
2 tablespoons lemon juice
1 tablespoon vanilla sugar (see note)
200 g (6 1/2 oz) fresh raspberries

**1** Preheat the oven to moderate 180°C (350°F/Gas 4). Beat the egg yolks and sugar in a small bowl until pale and creamy. Transfer to a large bowl and add the ricotta, pistachio nuts, lemon rind and juice and mix well.
**2** In a separate bowl, whisk the egg whites into stiff peaks. Beat in the vanilla sugar, then fold into the ricotta mixture, stirring until just combined.
**3** Lightly grease 4 individual, 1-cup (250 ml/8 fl oz) ramekins. Divide the raspberries among the dishes and spoon the ricotta filling over the top. Place on an oven tray and bake for 20–25 minutes, or until puffed and lightly browned. Serve immediately, dusted with a little icing sugar.

### COOK'S FILE

**Note:** You can buy vanilla sugar at the supermarket or make your own. Split a whole vanilla bean in half lengthways and place in a jar of caster sugar (about 1 kg/2 lb). Leave for at least 4 days before using.

*Beat together the egg yolks and sugar until pale and creamy.*

*Fold in the egg whites with a metal spoon, trying to keep the volume.*

*Put the raspberries in the ramekins and spoon the ricotta filling over the top.*

## HAZELNUT PUDDINGS WITH CHOCOLATE CREAM SAUCE AND HONEY ZABAGLIONE

Preparation time: 40 minutes
Total cooking time: 40 minutes
Serves 8

30 g (1 oz) butter, melted
1/2 cup (55 g/1¾ oz) ground
    hazelnuts
125 g (4 oz) butter
1/2 cup (125 g/4 oz) caster sugar
3 eggs, lightly beaten
2 cups (250 g/8 oz) self-raising
    flour, sifted
1/2 cup (60 g/2 oz) sultanas
1/3 cup (80 ml/2¾ fl oz) brandy
1/3 cup (80 ml/2¾ fl oz)
    buttermilk
white chocolate shavings, to
    decorate

*Chocolate Cream Sauce*
1 cup (250 ml/8 fl oz) cream
30 g (1 oz) butter
200 g (6½ oz) dark chocolate,
    chopped

*Honey Zabaglione*
3 large egg yolks
3 tablespoons honey
2 tablespoons brandy
1/2 cup (125 ml/4 fl oz) cream

**1** Preheat the oven to moderate 180°C (350°F/Gas 4). Brush eight, 1/2-cup (125 ml/4 fl oz) ovenproof ramekins with melted butter and coat with the ground hazelnuts, shaking off the excess. Beat together the butter and sugar with electric beaters until light and creamy. Add the eggs gradually, beating well after each addition.

Fold in the flour, sultanas, brandy and buttermilk. Spoon into the ramekins, cover with greased foil and secure with string.
**2** Place the puddings in a large baking dish and pour in enough water to come three-quarters of the way up the sides of the ramekins. Bake for 25 minutes, topping up with more water if necessary. Test with a skewer before removing the ramekins from the pan—the skewer should come out clean when inserted into the centre of the pudding.
**3 To make Chocolate Cream Sauce:** Put the cream, butter and chocolate in a small pan and stir over low heat until melted and smooth. Remove from the heat and set aside.
**4 To make Honey Zabaglione:** Beat the egg yolks until thick and pale. Place the bowl over a pan of barely simmering water and beat in the honey. Beat for about 5 minutes, until thickened. Remove from the heat, cool to room temperature and stir in the brandy. Beat the cream in a small bowl until firm peaks form, then fold into the egg mixture.
**5** Spread Chocolate Cream Sauce over half of each serving plate. Pour Zabaglione onto the other half. Unmould the warm pudding onto the centre of the plate and decorate with curls of white chocolate.

### COOK'S FILE

**Hint:** Make chocolate shavings by simply running over the top of the chocolate block with a vegetable peeler. Or make chocolate curls by melting the chocolate and spreading in a thin layer over a cool smooth surface (such as a marble board). When the chocolate has set, scrape off curls with the edge of a sharp knife.

*Brush the ramekins with melted butter then coat with ground hazelnuts.*

*Beat together the sugar and butter until light and creamy.*

*Cover the ramekins with foil and secure with string.*

*Pour water into the baking tray to make a bain-marie.*

*Put the bowl over a pan of simmering water and beat until thickened.*

*Unmould the puddings by working around the edges with a sharp knife.*

## STUFFED FIGS

Preparation time: 20 minutes
Total cooking time: 5 minutes
Makes 15

**50 g (1²/₃ oz) blanched almonds**
**15 soft dried figs**
**¹/₃ cup (60 g/2 oz) mixed peel**
**100 g (3¹/₃ oz) marzipan,**
**chopped**

**1** Preheat the oven to moderate 180°C (350°F/Gas 4). Place the almonds on an oven tray and bake for 5 minutes, until lightly golden. Leave to cool.
**2** Remove the hard stem ends from the figs. Cut a cross in the top of each fig halfway through to the base and open out like petals.
**3** Place the mixed peel and almonds in a food processor and process until fine. Add the marzipan and process in short bursts until fine and crumbly.

**4** With your hands, press 2 teaspoons of marzipan filling together to make a ball. Place a ball inside each fig and press back into shape around it. Serve at room temperature with coffee.

### COOK'S FILE

**Variation:** Dip the bases of the figs into melted chocolate.
**Storage time:** Store figs in a single layer in a covered container in the refrigerator for up to 2 days.

*Cut away the hard stem end from the bottom of each fig.*

*Cut a cross in the top and open out each fig like the petals of a flower.*

*Place a ball of marzipan filling in each fig and then remould the fruit around it.*

*Press the pastry into the base with your fingertips.*

*Line with baking paper and then fill with dried beans or rice to bake blind.*

*Push the ricotta through a sieve and then beat together with the sugar.*

*Fold the beaten egg white into the ricotta mixture with a metal spoon.*

## SICILIAN CHEESECAKE

Preparation time: 45 minutes + chilling
Total cooking time: 1 hour 25 minutes
Serves 8

2 cups (250 g/8 oz) plain flour
160 g (5¼ oz) butter, chopped
¼ cup (60 g/2 oz) caster sugar
1 teaspoon grated lemon rind
1 egg, lightly beaten

*Ricotta Filling*
½ cup (60 g/2 oz) raisins, chopped
⅓ cup (80 ml/2¾ fl oz) Marsala
500 g (1 lb) fresh ricotta
½ cup (125 g/4 oz) caster sugar
1 tablespoon plain flour
4 eggs, separated
½ cup (125 ml/4 fl oz) cream

**1** Lightly grease a 26 cm (10½ inch) round springform tin. Sift the flour and a pinch of salt into a large bowl and rub in the butter. Add the sugar, rind, egg and a little water if necessary and, using a knife, cut through until a rough dough forms. Press together into a ball.

**2** Roll out the dough on a lightly floured surface to line the base and side of the tin; chill for 30 minutes. Preheat the oven to moderately hot 190°C (375°F/Gas 5). Prick the pastry base, line with baking paper and fill with dried beans or rice. Bake for 15 minutes, then remove the beans and paper and bake for 8 minutes, or until pastry is dry. If the base puffs up, gently press down with the beans in the paper. Allow to cool. Reduce the oven to warm 160°C (315°F/Gas 2–3).

**3 To make Filling:** Put the raisins and Marsala in a small bowl, cover and leave to soak. Push the ricotta through a sieve. Beat the ricotta and caster sugar with a wooden spoon until combined. Add the flour and egg yolks, then the cream and undrained raisins and mix well. In a small bowl, beat the egg whites until soft peaks form and gently fold into the ricotta mixture in two batches.

**4** Pour the filling into the pastry case and bake for 1 hour, or until just set. Check during cooking and cover with foil if the pastry is overbrowning. Cool a little in the oven with the door ajar to prevent sinking. Serve warm with whipped cream.

*Beat together the egg yolks and sugar until thick and pale.*

*Fold the beaten egg whites into the cream mixture with a metal spoon.*

*Dip the biscuits into the coffee mixture and arrange in the serving dish.*

*Layer the remaining biscuits in the dish and spread over the cream mixture.*

## TIRAMISU

Preparation time: 30 minutes + chilling
Total cooking time: Nil
Serves 6–8

3 cups (750 ml/24 fl oz) strong
   black coffee, cooled
3 tablespoons dark rum
2 eggs, separated
3 tablespoons caster sugar
250 g (8 oz) mascarpone
1 cup cream (250 ml/8 fl oz),
   whipped
16 large savoyardi biscuits
2 teaspoons dark cocoa powder

**1** Put the coffee and rum in a bowl. Using electric beaters, beat the egg yolks and sugar in a small bowl for 3 minutes, or until thick and pale. Add the mascarpone and beat until just combined. Fold in the whipped cream with a metal spoon.

**2** Beat the egg whites until soft peaks form. Fold quickly and lightly into the cream mixture with a metal spoon, trying not to lose the volume.

**3** Dip half the biscuits, one at a time, into the coffee mixture; drain off any excess and arrange in the base of a deep serving dish. Spread half the cream mixture over the biscuits.

**4** Dip the remaining biscuits and repeat the layers. Smooth the surface and dust liberally with cocoa powder. Refrigerate for 2 hours, or until firm, to allow the flavours to develop. Delicious served with fresh fruit.

### COOK'S FILE

**Storage time:** Tiramisu may be made up to 8 hours in advance. Refrigerate until required.

## ESPRESSO GRANITA

Preparation time: 20 minutes +
    freezing
Total cooking time: 5 minutes
Serves 6

3/4 cup (185 g/6 oz) caster sugar
1 1/2 tablespoons cocoa powder
5 cups (1.25 litres) freshly
    made, strong espresso coffee
whipped cream, to serve

**1** Put the sugar and cocoa powder in a large pan, gradually add 1/2 cup (125 ml/4 fl oz) water and mix until smooth. Bring to the boil, stirring until the sugar dissolves. Reduce the heat and simmer for 3 minutes.
**2** Remove from the heat and add the fresh coffee. Pour into a shallow container or tray and allow to cool completely. Freeze until partially set and then stir with a fork to distribute the ice crystals evenly. Freeze again until firm.

**3** Using a fork, work the Granita into fine crystals and return to the freezer for 1 hour before serving. Spoon into glasses and serve immediately, with whipped cream.

### COOK'S FILE

**Hint:** The mixture does tend to freeze rock-hard which is why it should be put into a shallow tray and broken up when partially frozen. It can be quite difficult to break up if frozen in a deep container.

*Put the sugar and cocoa powder in a large pan and gradually add the water.*

*Remove the pan from the heat and pour in the fresh coffee.*

*Use a fork to work the Granita into fine crystals, then re-freeze for 1 hour.*

# BISCUITS

### FLORENTINES

Preheat the oven to moderate 180°C (350°F/Gas 4). Line an oven tray with baking paper. Sift ¼ cup (30 g/1 oz) plain flour into a bowl. Add 2 tablespoons each of chopped walnuts, chopped flaked almonds, finely chopped glacé cherries and finely chopped mixed peel and stir to combine. Combine 75 g (2½ oz) butter and ¼ cup (45 g/1½ oz) soft brown sugar in a pan, stirring over low heat until the butter has melted and the sugar dissolved. Add to the bowl and mix until just combined. Drop heaped teaspoonsful of the mixture onto the tray, leaving about 6 cm (2½ inches) between each. Press into neat 5 cm (2 inch) rounds. Bake for 7 minutes, then cool on the tray for 5 minutes. Lift carefully onto a wire rack to allow to cool completely. Repeat with the remaining mixture. Spread one side of each Florentine with melted dark chocolate and leave until set. Makes 24.

### PANFORTE

Preheat the oven to moderate 180°C (350°F/Gas 4). Brush a 20 cm (8 inch) round cake tin with oil or melted butter and line the base with baking paper. Combine ⅔ cup (90 g/3 oz) each of slivered almonds, chopped macadamia nuts and chopped walnuts in a large bowl with 1½ cups (285 g/9¼ oz) mixed dried fruit. Sift together ⅔ cup (85 g/2¾ oz) plain flour, 2 tablespoons cocoa powder and 1 teaspoon ground cinnamon and add to the bowl. Stir 60 g (2 oz) butter, 60 g (2 oz) chopped dark chocolate, ⅓ cup (90 g/3 oz) caster sugar and ¼ cup (90 g/3 oz) honey together in a small pan over low heat until melted and combined. Add to the dry ingredients and stir until just combined. Spoon into the tin and smooth the surface. Bake in the preheated oven for 50 minutes and then leave to cool completely in the tin before turning out. Dust with icing sugar and cut into thin wedges to serve. Makes 25 wedges.

*Biscuits from left: Florentines; Panforte; Chocolate Wafers; Biscotti; Amaretti*

## BISCOTTI

Preheat the oven to warm 160°C (315°F/Gas 2–3). Lighly oil a large oven tray and line with baking paper. Beat 3 eggs, 1 cup (250 g/8 oz) caster sugar and 1 teaspoon vanilla essence with electric beaters for 2 minutes, or until light and frothy. Sift in 2½ cups (310 g/9¾ oz) plain flour, ½ cup (60 g/2oz) self-raising flour, 1 teaspoon bicarbonate of soda and a pinch of salt and add ¾ cup (115 g/3¾ oz) toasted almonds. Mix with a knife to a soft dough. Divide into 3 portions and roll into log shapes about 20 cm (8 inches) long. Place on the tray and bake for 50 minutes. Cool on a wire rack. Cut the logs into thin slices, place on the tray and bake for 8 minutes each side. Cool and serve. Makes 50.

## CHOCOLATE WAFERS

Preheat the oven to slow 150°C (300°F/Gas 2) and line 3 oven trays with baking paper. Finely chop ⅔ cup (100 g/3⅓ oz) almonds. Finely chop 100 g (3⅓ oz) dark chocolate and add to the almonds with ½ teaspoon each of finely grated orange and lemon rind. Beat 2 egg whites with a pinch of salt until soft peaks form. Gradually add ½ cup icing sugar, beating well after each addition, until thick and glossy. Fold gently into the nut mixture. Place heaped teaspoonsful of the mixture on the trays and spread into 5 cm (2 inch) rounds. Bake for 20 minutes, until crisp and lightly coloured. Cool on the trays. Makes 30.

## AMARETTI

Line 2 baking trays with baking paper. Finely grind 125 g (4 oz) blanched almonds in a food processor and then mix in a bowl with ½ cup (125 g/4 oz) caster sugar. Whisk an egg white until frothy and add almost all to the almond mixture; stir to form a dough that is stiff, but soft enough to pipe (add more of the egg white if necessary). Spoon the mixture into a piping bag with a large nozzle and pipe small discs a little apart on the trays. Sift over a little icing sugar and press an almond into the centre of each. Leave, uncovered, for 4 hours at room temperature. Preheat the oven to slow 150°C (300°F/Gas 2). Bake for 25 minutes, or until lightly browned, and then cool on the trays. Makes about 35.

## CHOCOLATE RICOTTA TART

Preparation time: 20 minutes + chilling
Total cooking time: 1 hour
Serves 8–10

1½ cups (185 g/6 oz) plain flour
100 g (3⅓ oz) cold butter, chopped
2 tablespoons caster sugar
1 tablespoon butter, melted

*Filling*
1.25 kg (2½ lb) ricotta cheese
½ cup (125 g/4 oz) caster sugar
2 tablespoons plain flour
125 g (4 oz) chocolate, finely chopped

2 teaspoons coffee essence
4 egg yolks
40 g (1⅓ oz) chocolate, extra
½ teaspoon vegetable oil

**1** Make sweet shortcrust pastry by sifting the flour into a large bowl and adding the butter. Rub the butter into the flour with your fingertips, until fine and crumbly. Stir in the sugar. Add 3 tablespoons cold water and cut with a knife to form a dough, adding a little more water if necessary. Turn out onto a lightly floured surface and gather together into a ball. Brush a 25 cm (10 inch) springform tin with melted butter. Roll out the dough to line the tin, coming about two-thirds of the way up the side. Cover and refrigerate while making the filling.

**2 To make Filling:** Mix together the ricotta, sugar, flour and a pinch of salt until smooth. Stir in the chocolate, coffee essence and yolks until well mixed. Spoon into the chilled pastry shell and smooth. Chill for 30 minutes, or until firm. Preheat the oven to moderate 180°C (350°F/Gas 4).
**3** Put the tin on a baking tray. Bake for 1 hour, or until firm. Leave to cool before removing the sides from the tin. Melt the extra chocolate and stir in the oil. With a fork, flick thin drizzles of melted chocolate over the tart. Cool completely before cutting.

### COOK'S FILE

**Note:** The tart may crack during baking but this will not be noticeable when it cools and is decorated.

*Have cool hands and use just your fingertips when rubbing butter into flour.*

*Do not knead the dough or it will become tough—just gather it together into a ball.*

*Mix together the melted chocolate and oil and flick over the tart.*

*Cut the egg yolks into the dry ingredients with a knife.*

*Put the raisins in a bowl, pour over the orange juice and leave to soften.*

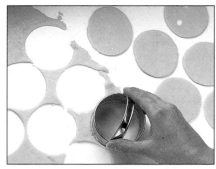

*Divide the dough in half to make it easier to handle. Cut out rounds with a cutter.*

*Place the filling in the centre of the pastry round and then fold over to enclose.*

## FRUITY NUT PASTRIES

Preparation time: 1 hour + chilling
Total cooking time: 20 minutes
Makes 40

2¹/2 cups (310 g/9³/4 oz) plain
 flour
165 g (5¹/2 oz) butter, chopped
¹/2 cup (125 g/4 oz) caster sugar
2 eggs plus 1 yolk, beaten
2 teaspoons lemon juice
1 egg yolk, lightly beaten, extra
1 tablespoon demerara sugar

*Fruit and Nut Filling*
125 g (4 oz) dried figs
75 g (2¹/2 oz) raisins
2 tablespoons fresh orange juice
75 g (2¹/2 oz) walnuts, finely
 chopped
100 g (3¹/3 oz) blanched, roasted
 almonds, finely chopped
2 tablespoons marmalade
1¹/2 tablespoons grated orange
 rind
¹/4 teaspoon ground cloves
1 teaspoon ground cinnamon

**1** Sift the flour into a bowl and rub in the butter with your fingertips. Stir through the sugar, then add the eggs and yolk and cut through with a knife to combine; add enough lemon juice to form a dough. Gather together into a ball, cover with plastic wrap and refrigerate for about 30 minutes.
**2 To make Fruit and Nut Filling:** Chop the figs, cover with boiling water and leave for 15 minutes to soften. Put the raisins in a bowl, cover with orange juice and leave for 15 minutes to soften. Drain the figs and raisins and combine in a bowl with the remaining filling ingredients.
**3** Preheat the oven to moderate 180°C (350°F/Gas 4). Cut the dough in half to make it easier to work with. Roll out each half to about 5 mm (1/4 inch) thick on a lightly floured surface and cut rounds, using an 8 cm (3 inch) cutter. Spoon 1 full teaspoon of filling into the centre of each round, brush the edges lightly with water and fold over to enclose the filling.
**4** Place on a lightly greased oven tray, brush with extra egg yolk and sprinkle with demerara sugar. Make cuts across the top of each pastry. Repeat with the remaining dough and filling. Bake for 20 minutes, or until lightly browned.

## ALMOND CITRUS TART

Preparation time: 40 minutes + chilling
Total cooking time: 1 hour
Serves 6–8

2 cups (250 g/8 oz) plain flour,
   sifted
1/4 cup (60 g/2 oz) caster sugar
125 g (4 oz) butter, softened
1 teaspoon finely grated lemon
   rind
2 egg yolks

*Filling*
350 g (11 1/4 oz) fresh ricotta,
   sieved
1/3 cup (90 g/3 oz) caster sugar
3 eggs, well beaten
1 tablespoon grated lemon rind
1/2 cup (80 g/2 2/3 oz) blanched
   almonds, finely chopped
3 tablespoons flaked almonds
icing sugar, to dust

**1** Combine the flour, sugar and a pinch of salt in a large bowl. Make a well in the centre and add the butter, rind and yolks. Work the flour into the centre with the fingertips of one hand until a smooth dough forms (add a little more flour if necessary). Wrap in plastic wrap and chill for 1 hour.
**2 To make Filling:** Using electric beaters, beat the ricotta and sugar together. Add the eggs gradually, beating well after each addition. Add the rind, beating briefly to combine, and then stir in the chopped almonds.
**3** Preheat the oven to moderate 180°C (350°F/ Gas 4). Brush a 20 cm (8 inch) deep fluted flan tin with melted butter. Roll out the pastry on a lightly floured surface and line the prepared tin, removing the excess pastry. Pour in the filling and smooth the top. Sprinkle with the flaked almonds and bake for 55 minutes to 1 hour, or until lightly golden and set.

**4** Cool to room temperature and carefully remove the sides from the tin. Dust with icing sugar to serve at room temperature or chilled.

*For perfect pastry, use just your finger-tips to bring the dough together.*

*Add the grated lemon rind and beat briefly to combine.*

*Roll a rolling pin over the lined tin to remove any excess pastry.*

## LEMON SYRUP CAKE

Preparation time: 20 minutes
Total cooking time: 45 minutes
Serves 8

1 cup (125 g/4 oz) plain flour
3/4 teaspoon baking powder
1/4 teaspoon bicarbonate of soda
50 g (1²/3 oz) unsalted butter
1/2 cup (125 g/4 oz) caster sugar
2 eggs
1/3 cup (80 ml/2³/4 fl oz) milk

3 tablespoons ground almonds
2 tablespoons grated lemon rind

*Syrup*
100 g (3¹/3 oz) caster sugar
1/3 cup (80 ml/2³/4 fl oz) fresh
  lemon juice

**1** Preheat the oven to moderate 180°C (350°F/Gas 4). Grease and line a 20 cm (8 inch) springform tin. Sift the flour, baking powder, bicarbonate of soda and a pinch of salt into a bowl.
**2** In a separate bowl, beat the butter,

sugar and eggs until light and creamy (the mixture may appear curdled). Fold in the flour mixture, then gently stir in the milk, almonds and lemon rind. Spoon into the tin and bake for 30–35 minutes, or until a skewer comes out clean. Make holes in the top of the cake with the skewer.
**3 To make Syrup:** Put the sugar and lemon juice in a small pan and stir over a low heat until syrupy; keep warm. Pour the syrup over the hot cake. Cool on a wire rack, then turn out of the tin to serve.

*Fold in the flour mixture, then gently stir in the milk, almonds and lemon rind.*

*Use a skewer to make holes in the top of the cake so it absorbs the syrup.*

*Pour the syrup over the hot cake, so that it is absorbed. Cool before turning out.*

## HONEY NUT ROLLS

Preparation time: 25 minutes
Total cooking time: 35 minutes
Serves 8

2 cups (250 g/8 oz) plain flour
1/4 cup (60 g/2 oz) caster sugar
100 g (3 1/3 oz) cold butter,
    chopped
4 tablespoons honey, warmed
3 tablespoons chopped almonds
3 tablespoons chopped pecans

1 teaspoon ground cinnamon
1/3 cup (60 g/2 oz) mixed peel,
    chopped
3 tablespoons chopped mixed
    almonds and pecans, extra

**1** Preheat the oven to moderate 180°C (350°F/Gas 4). Put the flour, sugar, butter and a pinch of salt in a bowl. Rub in the butter until crumbly. Add 2–3 tablespoons cold water and cut through, until the mixture forms a dough. Gather together into a ball.
**2** Cut the dough in half and roll each

piece into a strip about 40 cm x 10 cm (16 x 4 inches). Trim the edges with a knife. Spread 3 tablespoons honey over the dough and sprinkle with nuts, cinnamon and mixed peel. Roll up lengthways into two long sausage shapes and cut these in four. Place on a greased or paper-lined baking tray.
**3** Glaze with the remaining honey, sprinkle with mixed nuts and make diagonal slashes in the top. Bake for 35 minutes, or until golden brown. Serve warm with whipped cream, perhaps dusted with icing sugar.

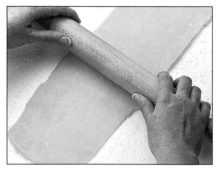

*Roll out each piece of dough into a long narrow strip.*

*Spread with honey, sprinkle with nuts, cinnamon and peel and then roll up.*

*Sprinkle with mixed nuts and then make a few diagonal slashes in the top.*

*Cut the slab sponge cake into 12 curved pieces with a sharp knife.*

*Put the thin ends of the cake slices in the centre so they fit together neatly.*

*Spoon the chocolate and hazelnut cream into the centre cavity and pack firmly.*

*Make a cardboard template and enlist help to give the Zuccotto a fancy finish.*

## ZUCCOTTO

Preparation time: 1 hour + chilling
Total cooking time: Nil
Serves 6–8

1 slab sponge cake, about
  30 x 25 cm (12 x 10 inches)
1/3 cup (80 ml/2³/4 fl oz) Kirsch
3 tablespoons Cointreau
1/3 cup (80 ml/2³/4 fl oz) rum,
  Cognac, Grand Marnier or
  maraschino
2 cups (500 ml/16 fl oz) cream
90 g (3 oz) dark roasted almond
  chocolate, chopped
3/4 cup (165 g/5¹/2 oz) finely
  chopped mixed glacé fruit
100 g (3¹/3 oz) dark chocolate,
  melted
70 g (2¹/3 oz) roasted hazelnuts,
  chopped
cocoa powder and icing sugar, to
  decorate

**1** Line a 6-cup (1.5 litre) pudding basin with damp muslin. Cut the cake into 12 curved pieces with a sharp knife. Work with one strip of cake at a time, lightly brushing it with the combined liqueurs and arranging the pieces closely in the basin. Put the thin ends in the centre so the slices cover the base and side. Brush with the remaining liqueur to soak the cake. Chill.

**2** Beat the cream into stiff peaks, then divide in half. Fold the almond chocolate and glacé fruit into one half. Spread evenly over the cake in the basin, leaving a space in the centre.

**3** Fold the cooled melted chocolate and hazelnuts into the remaining cream and spoon into the centre, packing firmly. Smooth the surface, cover and refrigerate overnight to allow the cream to firm slightly.

**4** Turn out onto a serving plate and decorate by dusting generously with cocoa powder and icing sugar. You can make a cardboard template to help you dust separate wedges neatly, although you may need help holding it in place. Serve immediately, as the cream mixture will soften quickly.

### COOK'S FILE

**Storage time:** Best made a day in advance to give the flavours time to develop while chilling.

## ICE CREAM CASSATA

Preparation time: 30 minutes + chilling
and overnight freezing
Total cooking time: Nil
Serves 8–10

250 g (8 oz) glacé fruit (such as
cherries, apricots or
pineapple), finely chopped
1/3 cup (40 g/1 1/3 oz) slivered
almonds, finely chopped
1/3 cup (80 ml/2 2/3 fl oz)
Cointreau or orange-
flavoured liqueur
2 litres good-quality vanilla ice
cream, softened slightly
1 1/4 cups (185 g/6 oz) unsalted
pistachio nuts, shelled and
finely chopped

**1** Cover the chopped glacé fruit and
almonds with the liqueur and soak for
10 minutes. Put a 9-cup (2.25 litre)
pudding basin in the refrigerator.
While the pudding basin is chilling,
divide the softened ice cream in half
and fold the pistachio nuts through
one half. If it begins to melt, return the
ice cream to the freezer until it is firm
enough to spread.
**2** When the basin is very cold, line it
with a layer of the pistachio ice cream
to three-quarters of the way up the
side (use a spoon, dipped in warm
water occasionally, to help spread it
evenly). Place in the freezer to re-set.
**3** Combine the remaining ice cream
with the soaked glacé fruit and
almonds. Mix until well combined.
(Return to the freezer if the ice cream
has softened too much to spread.)
Remove the basin from the freezer
and spoon in the ice cream and fruit
mixture. Smooth the surface and
return to the freezer overnight, or until
completely set.
**4** Turn out onto a chilled platter and
cut into wedges to serve.

### COOK'S FILE

**Storage time:** Will keep frozen for
up to one month.
**Hint:** An easy way to turn out the
Cassata is to lay a hot damp cloth
over the basin and keep reheating the
cloth until the basin lifts away. Try
not to melt the outside of the Cassata
too much.

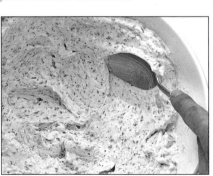

*Use a sharp knife to finely chop the glacé
fruit and slivered almonds.*

*Fold the pistachio nuts into half of the
softened ice cream.*

*Line the chilled basin with pistachio ice
cream, using a warm spoon to spread it.*

*Spoon the fruit ice cream into the centre
and return to the freezer to set.*

# INDEX

## INTERNATIONAL GLOSSARY

| | | | |
|---|---|---|---|
| bicarbonate of soda | baking soda | lima beans | butter beans |
| capsicum | red or green pepper | plain flour | all-purpose flour |
| caster sugar | superfine sugar | prawns, green | shrimp, raw |
| chickpeas | garbanzo beans | rocket | arugula |
| chilli | chili pepper, chile | semi-dried tomato | sun-blushed tomato |
| cream | single/light whipping cream | silver beet | Swiss chard |
| dark chocolate | plain chocolate | snow pea | mange tout |
| demerara sugar | raw sugar | spring onion | scallion |
| eggplant | aubergine | thick cream | double cream, heavy cream |
| egg tomato | plum/Roma tomato | tomato paste (Aus./US) | tomato purée, double concentrate (UK) |
| English spinach | spinach | tomato purée (Aus.) | sieved crushed tomatoes/passata (UK) |
| flat-leaf parsley | Italian parsley | | |
| ground almonds | almond meal | | |
| Nashi pear | Asian/Chinese/apple pear | zucchini | courgette |

This edition published in 2008 by Bay Books, an imprint of Murdoch Books Pty Limited.
Pier 8/9, 23 Hickson Road, Millers Point, NSW 2000, Australia

**Managing Editor:** Jane Price **Food Editors:** Kerry Ray, Tracy Rutherford
**Designer:** Wing Ping Tong **Recipe Development:** Amanda Cooper, Rosemary De Santis, Barbara Lowery, Sally Parker, Simitra Stais, Alison Turner
**Home Economist:** Michelle Lawton, Jo Richardson, Alison Turner
**Photographers:** Luis Martin, Reg Morrison (steps)
**Food Preparation:** Christine Sheppard **Food Stylist:** Mary Harris
**Chief Executive:** Juliet Rogers **Publisher:** Kay Scarlett

ISBN: 978 0 681 24487 0
Printed by Sing Cheong Printing Co. Ltd. PRINTED IN CHINA.